THE WAR AGAINST THE JEW

By the Same Author:

Concise Dictionary of Judaism
Dictionary of Philosophy
Hebrew Impact on Western Civilization
Letters to My God
Lost Legends of Israel
Of God, the Devil and the Jews
On the Nature of Man
Pictorial History of Philosophy
The Soviet Impact on Society
Treasury of Thought
The Wisdom of the Kabbalah

The War Against the Jew

by

Dagobert D. Runes

PHILOSOPHICAL LIBRARY
New York

To the memory of my mother,
victim of the fury of Anti-Semitic Prejudice

Raise not your children in disdain of Israel;
I say unto you, take out the venom from your
Scripture so that my people may live!

PREFACE

This is not a book of writings. This is a book of war.

There are many chronicles of war; of war lasting four days and of war lasting thirty years, even one hundred years, but then the war was over and peace followed.

My book is of a different war, a war forever, a war seemingly indissolubly attached to the creed of a billion people, a war that has become a dogma with the aggressor, a holy war with the most unholy consequences, a war deeply imbedded in the hearts of the bellicose, a war that never had an ending—even the rare armistices were not kept—a war so full of hate and cruelty for so long that history lacks any parallel, a war in which neither children nor invalids, the unarmed or ill, women or the aged, not even the newborn—who, our sages say, sleep in the wings of angels—were spared:

The War of the Christian Churches against the Jews!

This war is sometimes not declared but nonetheless pursued; when not pursued, the declaration still stands. Sometimes the war is cold,—cold hate preached in the Christian churches, seminaries and Sunday schools. The clergymen do not tell you whom to kill; they just tell you whom to hate.

Killing follows hate as combustion follows intense heat. The Christian clergymen start teaching their young at the tenderest age that *The* Jews killed the beloved gentle Son of God. That God Himself, the Father, punished *The* Jews by dispersion and the burning of their holy city. That God holds *The* Jews accursed forever and that the Romans (who had sacked every city in the Mediterranean cradle of civilization from Syracuse to Alexandria, from Carthage to Athens) tried to save the suffering Son of God, but the

Jews apprehended the child-loving Savior, insulted Him cruelly, beat Him, thorned Him and finally nailed Him to a cross. Indeed, the Jews even wished to break the dying God's bones.

This is no place to reason with faith.

Reason says that if a man or group of men have decided to judge and execute one of their own—even if their judgment be wrong, totally wrong—no one can be held to account but they themselves. Three out of four Hebrews did not live in Palestine at the advent of Jesus; nine out of ten of the Israelites in Palestine inhabited towns and villages outside the city of Jerusalem; and of the inhabitants of the holy city, only a few hundred could possibly even have heard the trial of Jesus on the hill of the Temple.

Why pursue with fire and sword the descendants of the few hundred, even were they guilty?

Why pursue the descendants of the Israelites who heard of the trial a hundred years later? Why pursue the descendants of the Israelites who lived a thousand miles away at the time of the trial?

Why pour vengeance on the innocent for thousands of years?

Vengeance for what? For being a member of *the* people chosen by God to give flesh to His Son; a people who gave Jesus a father who was named as His ancestor in body; a people who gave Jesus all His Apostles and Evangelists during His earth-living years?

Vengeance on the only people who listened to His words, the only people who believed in Him? Were they one hundred, or five thousand, Jews were the only followers of Jesus in His wanderings. He had none others He could speak to; He knew neither Greek nor Persian, Egyptian nor Roman. Hebrew and the vernacular Aramaic were all He spoke; it was God's tongue. As Jesus said, "I speak to my people in their synagogue."

His message was meant only for the Jews. No other nation expected or wished a Messiah (*Christos,* in Greek).

Any and all descendants of the kin and family of Jesus

shared the horrible fate of the dispersed Jews. They fought against the Romans led by Titus, and a hundred years later fought again under Bar Kochba against the enemy. It was then that half a million perished at the point of Rome's sword. Again, many of the defeated Jews fled north and west.

What became of the suffering wanderers from Israel? The kin of Joseph and Mary, no less than other Jews, suffered at the vengeful hands of the Christian oppressors. Later, one-third of the Jews of Spain were brutalized by the Catholic Inquisitors; one-third of the Jews of France were put to death by savage Catholics who libeled the people of God as blood drinkers, plague carriers, Host defamers and God killers. And much later, in our time, one-third of the Jews of the world were choked to death with noxious gases, by Protestant and Catholic Christians alike, in whom the fruit of the thousand-year-old teaching of Jew hate came to full bloom.

For all the two thousand years, there was no act of war against the Jews in which the Church did not play an intrinsic part. And wherever there was a trace of mercy, charity, or tolerance to be found amid this savagery, it came not from the Church but from humanitarians in the civil world, as in Napoleonic France or during the American Revolution.

America is the one and only Christian country that offered Jews freedom and security when the pyres were still flaming under the charred feet of Jewish women and children. Some fancy that these brutal outrages of the Catholic Church occurred only in the Dark Ages, as if this were an excuse. Nay, when George Washington was President, Jewish people were burning on the spit in Mexico.

However, need I remind anyone that the supreme holocaust took place only a few decades ago under the very eyes of Christian Europe; that the bishops of Austria and Germany blessed the arms of the killers, and the Vicar of Christ looked out of his window in Rome while Jewish children and women were dragged to extermination camps?

But the churches are not only guilty of ignoring the doom of a million Jewish children, choked to death along with their parents and grandparents.

The churches are guilty of directly inciting this massacre by their persistent religious teaching based on this thesis: *The* Jews killed God, therefore *all Jews* are damned.

Somehow, through the efforts of the one and only Pope free of Jew hate, John XXIII, the Jewish "problem" was put on the agenda of the Ecumenical Council. But the good Pope died and we were left with a former undersecretary of state of Pope Pius XII, the on-looker of Rome.

This new Pope, Paul VI, in 1965 in his Passion Sunday sermon, opened the Ecumenical Era with an alarming news report: The Prince of Peace was set upon by *the* (*sic!*) Jews; first *they* insulted Him, then *they* tortured and finally murdered Him.

This same Pope came in the fall of 1965 to New York, the greatest Jewish center of the world, and after a noble liturgy about peace on earth, touching on all nations of the world, he reserved for the Jews a brief reading: Jesus appeared after His agony to His disciples, who were assembled behind closed doors in fear of *the* (!) Jews.

Pope Paul VI further advanced Ecumenism by placing at the head of his Curia, charged with the task of "solving the Jewish problem," Bishop Luigi Carli of Segni, a professional anti-Semite during the Hitler era, a man whose outrageous behavior during the first sessions of the Council compelled even his conservative colleagues to stop his followers, the Carlifatti, from distributing racially poisonous literature to the delegates.

This monstrous man was put in charge of finding a "solution" to anti-Semitism.

He found one *for* anti-Semitism.

Carli's version of the noble schema proposed by John XXIII to absolve the Jews once and forever from the ridiculous generalization of Deicide, and to condemn anti-Semitism as a heresy, came out with a re-emphasis on the Jews as Christ killers and a sly "deploration" of anti-Semitism.

Carli won over John XXIII. Satan won over Christ.

To make certain that he was not being misunderstood, Carli followed his pronouncement with a lengthy article explaining that Judaism is condemned by God. Whoever follows Judaism cannot but be damnable.

Pope Paul's choice as head of the Ecumenical Curia also decreed that "all people of Israel were faithless" and that "the term deicide applied to all Jews is theologically faultless and the only apt definition."

It is doubly tragic to have to report that Pope Paul VI not only approved Carli's version of the Ecumenical declaration but actually sponsored it.

The fact that Vatican "liberals" managed to add to the vicious denunciation of *the* (*sic!*) Jew as Christ killer the sop, "Of course not all Jews of today are to be considered guilty of deicide," would be ludicrous were it not so tragic. No Catholic in his or her right mind ever considered the Jewish plumber across the street as being literally and specifically a killer of Jesus.

The farce is over and, the "Uncle Tom" Jews notwithstanding, the Vatican only *made believe* it had taken a great step toward the Jews' freedom from Catholic insolence and calumny!

The Vatican has merely taken a short step to the right and has cleverly sidestepped the cardinal issue: to cease once and forever teaching its youth that *the* Jew is a killer of God. And, furthermore it has sidestepped the issue of teaching its youth that anti-Semitism is a heresy and therefore damnable.

The Catholic Church has condemned Freemasonry but refuses to condemn Nazism.

It resolved that you cannot be a Catholic and a Mason, but you can still be a Catholic and a Nazi.

Perhaps Hitler was right when he exclaimed in 1933 at the Concordat Conference: "I am only continuing the work of the Catholic Church: to isolate the Jews and fight their influence."

*

xiii

The war of the Christian churches against the Jews began with the relentless attack of the early Church Fathers against the "stubbornness" of the Israelites who refused to accept Jesus as the Messiah. During the lifetime of Jesus a considerable number of Israelites followed Him—indeed, they were the only people who did. After His execution by the Romans who dominated the Palestine tip of Roman "Syria" with typical severity, Saul, a Talmudic student, and others began to develop a sect with grandiose mythological implications. Finding little acceptance for their unhebraic Christology and eschatology, they ignored the fact that the Messiah was to come to redeem Israel and Israel alone, and began to spread the gospel of the Messiah among the pagans.

Their propaganda was most effective, especially among the multitude of the lowly, and by the beginning of the fourth century Constantine, a pagan king, who had personally rejected the Christian faith, found it politically suitable to make Christianity the dominant and only religion for the whole Roman Empire, with the Bishop of Rome as its all-powerful head.

Among the citizens of Rome, patricians and equestrians alike took a highly sophisticated attitude toward the official Greek and Roman gods. They regaled themselves in word, song, and painting with the amours of Jupiter in the shape of a bull, swan, fish, even a cluster of coins. The plebeians, masses of proletarians, and slaves adhered to sundry traditional ritualistic customs which had as little firm theology as they had abundance of variation.

In this ocean of disbelief and superstition, the Jews were the only ones to maintain a *religio licita* in its true sense.

The Jews would not give up their spiritual heritage and faith in the guidance of the Torah. They did not accept Jesus as the Messiah, although they permitted evangelists, as they had permitted Jesus Himself, to preach in the synagogue.

They believed in one God, the Father of all, and the

Jewish people as His chosen servants. By this they were ready to live and by this they were ready to die.

In those crucial centuries of the growth of Christian religion from an obscure sect to the all-powerful Church of Rome, the early theologians of the Church turned about and opened the war against Israel.

Craving and finally getting Roman approval as *The* Church, they published papers and pamphlets, said prayers and delivered sermons making the Jews out to be the killers of Jesus, although in all Palestine's history there never was a single person crucified except by Romans, and by Romans alone. This being known, the early Church Fathers made the Jews the *instigators* of the Crucifixion. This suited them very well, since the Jews coldly rejected the Roman brand of Christianity, while the Romans, on the other hand, were expected to, and did grant the rapidly spreading Christian Church absolute religious power.

The early Church Fathers—Eusebius, Cyril, Chrysostom, Augustinus, Origen, Justin, Jerome—carried on a venomous campaign against the Jewish "killers of Jesus," and when the New Testament was finally put together, it was laced with anti-Semitic statements. Pilate, of course, was made out to be a gentle Roman judge. The police chief became the personification of eternal justice, *lex Romana.*

The Jews, on the other hand, as the Christian Gospels were made to read, were bloodthirsty persons, torturers of the Savior, pitiless killers, traitors who sold their souls for thirty pieces of silver, moneychangers who desecrated the Temple, more cruel than beasts in demanding that the bones of the dying Christ be broken—the Jews were the sons of the Devil.

Such was the propaganda campaign of the early Fathers of the Catholic and Orthodox Church. These inflamed charges, which they demanded be taken as gospel truth, were followed by admonitions to the secular powers to expel the Jews, to isolate them, to burn their synagogues, to destroy their Talmud and Torah.

These same Fathers also charged the Jews with drinking the blood of Christian children, with poisoning the food and water of true believers, with conspiring with the Asian enemies of the Christians, with desecrating churches and crucifixes, and so on.

The War against the Jews had begun. From pulpit to pulpit, every Sunday and holy day, in every Church of Christ, cold hate was released against the hapless Jewish families. And this teaching of hate has not ceased to this very day.

Soon the cold hate turned into fiery action, and from one end of Europe to the other the almighty Catholic Church put the Jews to the pyre and sword. No child, no woman, no invalid was spared.

The wretches who fled one bishop were soon overtaken by the mobs incited in another diocese. To make the victims easily recognizable they were made by the Catholic Church to wear the leper sign. They were corralled into foul ghettos, easy prey to the wanton cruelty of the sermon-crazed Christians.

Wild agitators of hate against the Jews, armed with supreme powers by the Church, were sent through all Christian lands. Wherever they passed, the pyres were built up, with whimpering flesh dying an agonized death at the hands of executioners with the big silver cross dangling from their necks.

Three and a half million Jews died in this Church War against the Jews. When Hitler embarked on the road to kill another six million of the people of the Lord, he found to his admitted amazement that his Eichmann and Kaltenbrunner were as little opposed by the Germans as Cardinals Jiménez and Torquemada of iniquitous memory had been by the Iberians.

The German Christians had centuries of preparation for Jew slaughter, first by the Catholic Church and then by the renegade monk Martin Luther, who wanted the "killers of Jesus" made slaves of the serfs, because they were the sons of the Devil and should never touch a free Christian's hand. Luther demanded that the synagogues be burned, the books of the Hebrews destroyed, and Jewish homes laid waste.

What Hitler did was only putting Luther's war plans into reality. Indeed, everything Hitler did to the Jews, all the horrible, unspeakable misdeeds, had already been done to the smitten people before by the Christian churches, especially the Catholic Church.

The isolation of Jews in ghetto camps, the wearing of the yellow spot, the burning of Jewish books, and finally the burning of the people—Hitler learned it all from the Catholic Church. However, the Church burned the Jewish women and children alive, while Hitler granted them a quicker death, choking them first with gas.

Yet all these horrible acts are only part of the evil done to the Jews. As in all wars, much of the bestiality remains forever hidden. Never has man been more cruel to man than the Christians have been to the Jews.

Will the infamy of this war ever end?

How can it, so long as the Christian churches continue to teach their youth that the Jews are the brood of the Devil and *the (sic!)* Jews are killers of their God?

How can this crime cease, so long as the churches tolerate anti-Semitism as a natural attitude of Christians and refuse to declare it sinful heresy?

The young Christians of today have been given the same lessons in hate as the young Christians a generation ago. The cold war teachings of anti-Semitism have not ceased. The Christians tomorrow will be as ready to fall upon the Jews as they were yesterday.

Neo-Nazism is again born out of Christianity. It is the same old teaching: the Jew is pariah. In Poland, in the Ukraine, in Argentina—wherever there are Christian churches there is anti-Semitism.

The Gospel of St. John, the teaching Gospel of the Christian churches, contains thirty-two references to the

Jews. Every one is meant to debase and degrade the Jew and make him hateful to the core. ("The Jew is the son of the Devil." John 8:44)

Rip out these sentences from your Gospels, for if your Gospels have to stand or fall by these few anti-Semitic lines, they certainly do not deserve to live on.

These sentences were put there by hate-maddened, primitive theologians of fifteen hundred years ago, and kept there by the power-seeking Bishops of Rome.

You have burned to ashes almost ten million of our people, a million of our children, because of your hate, and you are ready to burn more when the time is ripe, when the cold hate again turns into the flames of war.

Every Sunday of every week your youth is being readied for the supreme task of extermination. There is not a week when a Jewish cemetery or synagogue is not desecrated somewhere in the Christian world.

All reports and surveys make it clear that Christian youth overwhelmingly have a disdain or hate for Jews because of their religious training.

Make not your Church the headquarters of the war against the people of Jesus, Mary, and Joseph. You have burned to death one-third of their kin. Do you wish to burn the others?

The War against the Jews is almost two thousand years old, and still you continue your preparations for the next massacre!

I do not know where such an outbreak will take place. I did not know a few decades ago that it would happen in Germany.

I do not know where the next burning will occur. The air of Spain, of Portugal, of England, of Italy, of Germany, of Austria, of France, of Mexico, and of Brazil—the air of all holds the memory of burned Jewish flesh.

Do you really want to stop this massacre or do you want to be "neutral" like the Vicar of Christ, and then benignly say a prayer over the victims?

It is in your hands; we are only a few, among a billion Christians.

*

Some indifferent historians argue that, after all, the German Christians had to perform the Jew killings as a matter of enforced war duty; and all along that has been the alibi of the most sadistic concentration camp commanders. Of course the argument is as weak as the desire of those people to unmask the truth.

The truth is that Hitler, a graduate of the Linzer school of clerical anti-Semitism, was sure of his victory once the Catholic Church, through the untiring efforts of Pacelli, later Pius XII, joined him in the infamous Concordat of Collaboration, which turned the youth of Germany over to Nazism, and the churches became the stage background for the bloodthirsty cry: *"Pereat Judea!"*

The Protestants went them one better and, with hardly an exception, joined in a religious Fatherland Front. The most influential Bishop Müller even dedicated a sermon, which was widely publicized, to "Hitler and Christ." Of course, Christ came out second best.

To begin with, Hitler's desire to exterminate all Jews was on public record in his *Mein Kampf.* Pacelli knew that, as did all German Christians, in the pulpit or in the pew. Still, the German nation overwhelmingly voted for Hitler, and in Austria the Catholic Church through its Cardinal Innitzer openly asked its citizens to vote for union with Nazi Germany. Even before this "union" Innitzer signed his pastoral letters: "Heil Hitler." His painting in full regalia still decorates Catholic public buildings in Austria, the country that in the Middle Ages had burned alive hundreds of Jews.

Innitzer helped burn a thousand times that many.

The Christian Germans voted Hitler in—he was not a usurper—they followed him through his travels and festivals with delirious enthusiasm. There are a mass of street and stadium photographs available showing the Nazi killer exhorting the populace to Jew slaughter, with the faces of the Teutons shining with adoration for the beloved leader, and down in front there are always the Christian clergy with benign smiles on their lips.

It was the same smile on the faces of the priests of the Spanish Inquisition, taking down the whispered confessions of tortured Jews, the same smile on the face of Peter the Hermit crying for the blood of Jews during the march of the Crusader hyenas, the same smile on the bishops of England watching Jews being burned in York, the same smile on the monks in France accusing Jews of well-poisoning and plague-carrying, the same smile on the Ukrainian Orthodox priests watching Jews being sorted out and shot in Babi Yar.

The churches of Europe rang the bells when Hitler won a victory, as they rang throughout Germany whenever the last Jew of the town was deported to perdition.

The Church, however, was not a silent witness. The priests and ministers preached sermon after sermon, published in their religious as well as the commercial press, on the greedy, the usurious, the nefarious, the power-mad Jew —and, of course, as an undertone, on the Jews as crucifiers of Christ.

The Church was then, as it is now, the prime bearer of anti-Semitic tales, ancient and new.

The barbarism of the German Christians toward the Jews is the direct result of the teaching of the anti-Semitic Church. The Germans did not deliberately kill a single Christian child or woman.

The killing of Jews, child and adult, the Christian Germans carried out with indifference, indeed, often with a sense of pride. They had learned from childhood to regard the Jew as vermin, as the son of Satan. Killing Jews was a duty, advised during the Middle Ages again and again by the Church.

Hitler only carried out the avowed policy of the Christian Church. Because of his talent for organization and modern scientific acumen, he exceeded even the excesses of the Church.

Anti-Semitism begins with the Christian Church and can only end with it, certainly not without it.

Where is the first man of God among the Christians who will come forth in the name of Pope John XXIII and cry out, "We have sinned against the Jews by massacring the people of Jesus, and we have sinned as free men of the twentieth century by holding Jewish children responsible for a deed that may have been done two thousand years ago"?

Such men of courage and vision will come, and this book is meant to help them understand the gravity of their judicial crimes committed upon a little nation that has done no wrong except being the kin of Christ.

*

I say to the Catholic Church: Where are the Jews of Spain, of Portugal? You killed them. Where are the Jews of Italy, of France? You killed them. Where are the Jews of England? You killed them. Where are the Jews of Hungary and Austria? You killed them.

I say to the Protestants of Prussia and the Catholics of Bavaria: Where are the Jews of Germany? You killed them.

I say to the Orthodox of Russia and the Ukraine: Where are the Jews of the Czar? You killed them.

The Christian churches of Europe have killed and maimed the Jews from the days of the Visigoths to the pogrom in Kielce, Poland, in 1946.

If not for Cain with cross and sword, the Jewish nation would today comprise a hundred million people instead of fifteen million. As the centuries went by, Israel lost its majorities through conversion and the torch.

Will Cain ever face the Lord?

*

I am no respecter of the Cloth. Peter the Hermit wore the monk's hirsute shirt when he reviled the Jews as a brood out of hell and so opened the Crusade with the blessing of an ax over our people's heads.

Cardinal Torquemada wore the Cloth when he watched agonized victims of torture "confessing" to monstrous crimes.

Martin Luther wore the Cloth when he damned the Jews to slavery and to having their homes and temples and holy books burned.

Cardinal Innitzer of Vienna wore the Cloth when he asked the Austrians to join Hitler.

I call a spade a spade, not the less when I see it in the hands of my gravediggers.

*

The War against the Jews led by the Christian churches has for the time being shifted to a cold war. We Jews are standing now between outbreaks of open violence, as we stood between the various Crusades, as we stood between vampire trials and Black Death accusations, as we stood between the Count Rindfleisch campaign and the Hussite wars, as we stood between the Chmielnicki bloodbath and the Russian pogroms, as we stood between the Rumanian barbarism and the Nazi holocaust.

There has not been a century in which the churches have ceased their malevolent sermons against the Hebrews, the moneychangers, the killers of beloved Jesus, instilling in the children entrusted to them an eerie fear of and contempt of devils, these Shylocks, these Judases, these Jews.

How shall I speak of these dark men of the cross?

They were no better than the Nazis, merely less powerful, less thorough.

There is no town in any Christian land of Europe where the ministers of Christ have not incited and led the mob as well as the nobles and kings to burn the Jew!

The extermination camps of the German Christians were only the culmination of the holy terror that Catholic clergy conducted for fifteen hundred years.

Some say we should forgive. I can forgive them the killing of my mother but cannot forget the million little

xxii

ones they choked to death as you would not a cat or a dog.

They want us to forgive the killing of six million Jews—and cannot forgive us the alleged killing of one.

They did not even bury our dead. They burned them and threw the ashes into the dirt, the Catholic bishops no less than the Brown Shirts.

If these sanguinary men believed in God, they could not burn children or choke them or stamp them to death. They must be certain that God is dead and that they now hold His reins.

No believer in God can be as cruel, as merciless, as bestial, as the Catholic Church has been to us. No man can watch a million children choke to death and not raise a finger unless he has lost all faith, all faith forever!

As I write these lines, reports are coming in that the Neo-Nazi Party in Bavaria, the *Nationaldemokratische Partei Deutschlands,* has won over 10 percent of the votes of this Catholic province, with the priests giving their gains a benevolent consent; reports come from Warsaw that the Jews in Poland, whose schools are totally in the hands of the Catholic Church, are subject to constant derision and abuse as Christ killers; reports come from Kiev that the Orthodox Christians of this town have for twenty years been using the burial place of its Jewish population massacred by the Nazis, Babi Yar, as a dumping ground, and that the Jews, as in earlier papal days, are not permitted to build synagogues or raise their children in their faith, celebrate their holy days, or even read their prayer books; reports come from Catholic Argentina, which has become the haven of Nazi criminals, that the youth are infected by the clergy with anti-Semitic prejudices which frequently lead to hostile acts against the Jews; reports come from Protestant England that academic dictionaries of the English language, such as those of the Oxford University Press, have still not ceased defining Jew in the old church manner of Reverend Prynne as "cheats, usurers, unscrupulous bargainers."

It is too late to raise one's voice when the ax has fallen,

and it *will* fall again on the heads of our kinsmen if we do not succeed in persuading the Christian clergy to cease the teaching of contempt and hate for the Jew.

Cleanse your catechisms and cleanse your scriptures, I say, of the malevolent Roman references to our people.

Those who honestly wish to make an end to the scourge of anti-Semitism, be they Jew or liberal Gentile, let them speak out now and move to correct the vicious texts of the churches and make an end to the Jew-baiting sermonology!

Let us not sit out this cold war until the inevitable pogrom; let us fight now!

They are a billion strong, and we are few, but tomorrow is in the hands of the Lord.

*

I have chosen only sample events and personalities implicated in the wanton War against the Jews. My book makes no claim to completeness. One need not know the gory totality of the anti-Semitic carnage to be appalled by its magnitude.

Even an enumeration of all the known sanguinary occurrences would fall short; infamy often does its work in darkness and silence, unbeknown to the wide public.

How many Jews were subject to persecution in the two thousand years of Christian domination no one will ever know. But of what we know, I have endeavored to give you a brief record.

If the facts are abhorrent, there is much more I have refrained from advancing, to spare my people who read this book.

I fervently hope that enough liberals will be found among Christian theologians and ministers to reach the true depth of contriteness and set upon the great task of freeing Christian teachings of the sin of anti-Semitism.

For the serious student I have added a bibliography offering documentation.

No one has to hate the Jews in order to love Jesus.

A

ABRAHAM A SANTA CLARA (1644-1709)

wrote, when the Turkish invasion threatened Vienna and brought about general misery: "After the Devil the Christians have no greater enemy than the Jew. They pray daily that God destroy us by pestilence and famine. Are there any greater scoundrels than Jews?"

This vicious Augustinian monk mounted the pulpit in school and church to accuse the Jews of bringing the plague.

ABULAFIA, SAMUEL HA-LEVI (1320-1360)

Treasurer of Don Pedro of Castile. The Catholic clergy conspired against him and had him tortured to death.

ADVERSUS JUDAEOS

General term for anti-Semitic literature, especially that authored by the early Church Fathers. The most vicious of all was John Chrysostom (Saint) of the fifth century, who ran wild at the mouth against the Jews: "They are rapists, pushy, deceitful, hucksters." Further, they are: ". . . Lustful, rapacious, greedy, impure, debauchers. . . ." A worthy predecessor of the Nazi Streicher.

AGOBARD, SAINT (779-840)

Archbishop of Lyon who directed his church activities to spread anti-Semitism. In his essayistic epistles he

1

"proved" that the Jews were born slaves, were stealing Christian children and selling them to the Arabs, are accursed by God and should be so regarded by all Christians.

Again, many statements of this high-placed clergyman have found willing ears among modern anti-Semites.

AHLWANDT, HERMANN (b. 1846)

Journalistic anti-Semite of Prussia. Strongly supported by the Protestant clergy. Helped prepare ground for Nazism.

AKSAKOV, IVAN SERGEYEVICH (1823-1886)

Journalistic Russian anti-Semite, strongly supported by the Orthodox clergy.

AKTION REINHARD

The code name for the detailed plan to plunder the property of the Jews in Nazi Germany; so titled after its director, Reinhard Heydrich.

A guideline for this plan could be found in nation-wide expropriations by the Catholic Church in conjunction with various rulers. The Catholic Church provided many models for expropriation combined with execution or expulsion of Jews on repeated occasions. The Nazis merely streamlined an old operation.

ALBA, DUKE OF (1508-1582)

Repugnant anti-Semite of the Spanish aristocracy. Prohibited the printing of Hebrew books in the Netherlands. Similar prohibition is attributed to Joseph Stalin, a former Christian seminary student, who gave up the faith of his youth but not his anti-Semitic prejudices. The Stalin prohibition still holds good in the Soviet Union, minor exceptions for propaganda purposes to the contrary.

ALBERTUS MAGNUS (1206-1280)

A bishop of the Catholic Church and one of its revered philosophers, he presided over the tribunal that condemned the books of the Talmud in 1248 as pernicious literature. In the Hitler era German theologians often borrowed quotations from this "trial," such as "Talmud Jews."

ALBI

In this French town in 1320 the total Jewish population was annihilated by the Catholic authorities.

ALBRECHT OF BRANDENBURG

This Roman Catholic Archbishop initiated in 1516 a movement to expel all Jews from Germany. He was only partly successful. Completion of the pious task had to wait almost five hundred years.

ALEXANDER I (1777-1825)

Czar of the Russians who expelled the Jews from villages to certain restricted towns and forbade them to keep Christian servants (August 10, 1824 and January 13, 1825). A reversion to the anti-Semitic attitudes of medieval Catholicism.

ALEXANDER III (1845-1894)

The anti-Semitic attitude of this Russian Czar was manifest. As soon as he ascended the throne pogroms broke out in 160 places. Jewish women were publicly outraged, and thousands of persons of the Hebrew faith were mutilated or killed and their property put to the torch. The clergy of Russian Orthodoxy spread the terror, finding it opportune to sermonize on the Christ killers.

In Warsaw persecution of the Jews began on Christmas,

1881, as an aftermath of Church services. The military as well as the civilian authorities were so deeply imbued since childhood with anti-Semitism that instead of protecting the Jews they turned against them.

As usual, unscrupulous opportunists turned to anti-Semitism as a means for blackmail, and solicitation of funds from wealthy Jew haters.

In 1890, American liberals appealed to Czar Alexander to give the Jews access to economic opportunity in the arts, crafts and professions, and freedom to move about, since their condition was the most wretched of all people in Europe. The pious ruler quoted a sentence from the Patriarch of Kiev: "Let us never forget that *the Jews* [*!*] crucified our Lord and spilled His precious blood."

What piety and nobility—almost matched by that other Alexander III, the Pope (1159-1181), who reproved King Louis VII of France for treating the "killers of the Savior" like Christians.

A thousand miles away, a thousand years apart—yet but one thought in two namesakes united by the bonds of faith.

ALFONSO X (1252-1284)

Under this Castilian King, the Seven Part Code (*Las siete partidas*) was devised by the Catholic hierarchy. One part reads: "We order that no Jews shall dare to bathe in company with Christians."

The exclusion of Jews from Castilian beaches and baths intrigued Hitler. He made the Castilian Code valid for Germany. In later years, however, in Catholic Spain as in Nazi Germany, Jews were to be found only in cemeteries.

ALFONSO DE SPINA

Noted Spanish theologian, who proved (in his book *Fortalitium fidei*) by the Talmud itself that the Jews were children of the Devil.

4

ALGIERS

When anti-Semitic mobs attacked the Jewish shops in Algiers (February, 1898), *La Croix,* a leading Catholic newspaper in France, claimed that Christ Himself had protected the Christian shops. Did the devout fathers who edited *La Croix* know that the Jewish shops of Algiers had been marked the night before with a white Star of David?

The marking of Jewish places of business was successfully used by the Brown Shirts fifty years later. Did Christ protect the Christian shops in Berlin?

AMBROSE, SAINT

A fourth-century bishop of Milan and one of the four Latin Doctors of the Catholic Church, he reprimanded Emperor Theodosius for ordering the rebuilding of a synagogue in Mesopotamia that had been destroyed by a monk-led mob. In his zeal the good saint himself offered to burn the synagogue in Milan. Unfortunately other Christians had done so already.

AMULO

This Bishop of Lyon (841-852), successor of the notorious Agobard was also a prolific epistle writer. He claimed like our present-day Bishop Luigi Carli (who, for God knows what reason, was placed by the Vatican at the head of the four-man Curia committee to offer a "Schema on the Jews"), that the Mosaic religion was an accursed faith. His vile references to the Jews were often used by the German Jew haters.

ANJOU

In this French city in the years 1236, 1239, and again in 1271, thousands of Jews were put to the sword by monk-accompanied Crusaders. Contemporary chronicles describe the monstrous events.

ANSBACH

The Jewish population of this Bavarian town was put to death in 1349 by flagellants singing hymns of Christian love. Not one Jew escaped.

ANTICHRIST

is depicted by the clergy from the thirteenth century on as an offspring of Jews, and supported by Jews, who, with Satan's guidance, would destroy the true faith and re-establish Judaism as the dominant power. In medieval illustrations and plays, the Devil wears the Jew badge, has a hook nose and curly hair.

ANTI-SEMITISM

This term is first found in *Der Sieg des Judenthums über das Germanenthum* ("The Victory of Judaism over Germanism") by Wilhelm Marr (1879).

ANTI-SEMITISM IN ABSENTIA

is one of the many facts in evidence that Jew hate is hardly ever caused by the specific acts or behavior of Jews in the community, but rather by the deplorable educational process of the Christian church. Indeed, the three most anti-Semitic countries in recent decades are Austria, Poland and Bavaria. None of these Catholic lands now have any Jewish residents to speak of, yet the majority of the rural youth of Austria, Poland and Bavaria, who have most likely never seen a Jew, never competed against one, or been hurt or affected by one, carry hearts full of hate for "the Christ killers."

Similarly, for many centuries the populace of England,

Spain, Portugal, and other lands where the Jews had been expelled or put to death, retained a blind fury against the "children of the Devil," who "tortured their Savior."

All that these Christians, young or old, knew of the Jew was what they learned from their liturgy, but this was enough to set their minds in perpetual hate. It is not the presence of Jews that creates anti-Semitism, rather the persistence of Gospel teachings in their hate-instilling form.

We find the same situation in all of Western and Southern Europe in the early part of the eighteenth century. Those among the Jews who escaped the fury of the Church had fled to the Moslem countries, or to the "under-developed" Russian East, where Jewish skills and know-how were needed. Yet, in spite of the small number of Jews left in such countries as Germany, France, Italy, Spain, England and Switzerland, the Church managed to keep the issue of anti-Semitism alive by repeating again and again, from pulpit and printing press, the great lies of the Jews being God killers, the Jews profaning the host, the Jews being vampires, the Jews being poisoners of the very wells they were themselves using, the Jews bringing the plague to the very same streets they themselves were frequenting, the Jews bringing the Mongols and Moslems to destroy the Christian Church, and so on.

As stupid as these and the other anti-Semitic fabrications sound today, nevertheless, the populace of Europe— illiterate for the most part, and those few literate confused and browbeaten by the fanatics and power-mongers of the dominant Church—the populace absorbed Jew hate and acted upon it at the pleasure of Dominicans, Franciscans and the malevolent Vatican itself.

If there was any lull in the anti-Semitism of the first eighteen centuries of Christianity, it came from secular sources, never from the Church.

APULIA

In this district of Southern Italy the Dominican order in the fourteenth century destroyed all Jewish cemeteries and converted the synagogues into churches.

The Jewish population was given the choice of baptism or the stake by King Charles I. Eight thousand accepted conversion, the others fled.

AQUINAS, SAINT THOMAS

Catholic philosopher (1227-1274), defender of slavery for Jews, who wrote: "The Jews refuse to work, they never do anything, that's why they become more and more avaricious."

ARAGON

In this province of Spain in the fourteenth century thousands of Jews were either baptized or killed. Under King Martin, those who remained alive after the bloody excesses of Father Vincente Ferrer had to wear the badge and destroy their Hebrew books.

The schismatic Pope Benedict XIII, forced to seek refuge in his native Aragon, in 1415 issued a bull *Etsi Doctoribus Gentium* that barred Jews from holding any office or following the profession of physician, chemist or merchant. All Jews over the age of twelve were required to listen to proselytizing sermons three times a year.

ARBRIES, PEDRO (1441-1485)

A Spanish canon, one of the most fiendish inquisitors into faith. He was finally assassinated by a Marrano. Pope Pius IX canonized this monster (1867).

ARGENTINA

Today anti-Semitism as represented by Tacuara is running along "Christian" lines. Its spiritual head is the Catholic priest Dr. Alberto Contreras. Nazi-type mass meetings with Hitler salute, etc., are held in front of the Cathedral of St. Francis with full knowledge of the Archbishop.

ARLES

In this French city on April 8, 1484, mobs led by monks attacked the Jews, compelled about fifty to accept Christianity, and murdered the rest. Contemporary chronicles hail this "victory for Christ."

ARMLEDER

A murderous group in Alsace, under the leadership of John Zimberlin, who took it upon themselves in the fourteenth century to avenge the crucifixion by cutting down Jews. Their outrages were only a prelude to the Black Death massacres in Central Europe.

ARNOLD OF CITEAUX

A protégé of Pope Innocent III (1198-1216), this Cistercian monk, at the head of a crusading army against the Albigenses, killed 200 Jews of Béziers in France. A few in despair grabbed for the Crucifix to escape death.

ARYAN CHRISTIANITY

In a pastoral letter of 1939 Archbishop Konrad Gröber argued that Jesus was totally different from the Jews and therefore they crucified Him.

Bishop Hilfrich of Limburg "reasoned" that Christianity was not to be regarded as a product of Israel; it was therefore not un-German. In fact, it finds itself in intimate union with the German spirit. (1939 Pastoral letter).

These and similar articles, as well as books of Christian anti-Semitism, bore the imprimatur. Bishop Alois Hudal, head of the German church in Rome, declared that the Nuremberg Laws were a necessary self-defense against the influx of Jewish elements into Christian Germany.

ATHANASIUS, SAINT

A fourth-century bishop of Alexandria, honored as the father of orthodoxy; insisted that Rome use the sword to deal with the Jews and that tolerance toward Jews was treason against Christ.

AUGUSTINE, SAINT (354-430)

Bishop of Hippo and the most influential Catholic theologian, he called Judaism a corruption. "The true image of the Hebrew is Judas Iscariot, who sells the Lord for silver. The Jew can never understand the Scriptures and forever will bear the guilt for the death of Jesus."

In the judgment of this fountain of Christian love, the Jew must forever spend his life as a slave.

AUSSEE

In this Austrian town in 1722 the synagogue was burned down by orders of the Catholic Church because a priest who had entered the house of worship uninvited on Jewish High Holy Days, was prevented from delivering a conversion sermon.

AUSTRIA

This little Catholic state can justly claim the dubious distinction of being for one hundred years the most anti-Semitic country of Europe. Austria is not only the homeland of Adolf Hitler, but the stamping ground of such professional Jew baiters as Father August Rohling, Georg von Schoenerer and Karl Lueger, who, with the help of the clerical organizations and press, worked for the exclusion of the Jews from all economic and cultural life. The Jew was depicted as a monstrous creature from the pulpits of the many Catholic churches of Austria and of course received similar treatment in the clerical press, from the *Reichspost* of Vienna to a precursor of *Der Stürmer* called *Kikeriki.*

This type of propaganda found willing listeners among the Church-educated Austrians, who elected the candidate of the clergy, Karl Lueger, as Mayor of Vienna, and swamped the Austrian Parliament with Jew haters (1897).

As late as 1925 the deans of all Austrian universities and schools of higher education passed a resolution that no Jews be given academic posts.

Today these same universities and schools of higher education, which have for a hundred years been a hotbed of Jew hate, are still deeply infected with anti-Semitic clericalism. One of its most virulent representatives is the Catholic lay leader, Taras Borodajkewycz, Professor of Social History at the Viennese College of Commerce, who, despite—or because of?—his pre-Hitler Nazi background received and retained his important post. I was in his classroom in March of 1965 when, during one of his tirades against world Jewry, Austrian students took up the cry: "Out with the Jews!" and "Long live Auschwitz!—(*Lang lebe Auschwitz!*)" This same Borodajkewycz is one of the contributing editors of the academic monthly *Eckartsbote,* which is no less anti-Semitic than the *Deutsche Hochschullehrer Zeitung.*

In 1965 the University of Vienna appointed the Nazi Helfried Pfeiffer professor of history. Pfeiffer wrote in 1941: "Hitler was Austria's greatest son." Pfeiffer's lecture series in 1965 was entitled "The Essence of Democracy."

The treatment of Nazi criminals in Austria has naturally been most lenient. In 1961, of sixteen mass killers tried, eleven were acquitted and the others released after having received token sentences. At almost every trial, however, an invited public was loudly expressing its resentment of Jewish "vengeance seekers."

Of the top judges who presided during the Hitler era over "Special Courts" of extermination, one is professor of law at the University of Innsbruck; another became co-author of the Penal Code of the "new Austria."

AUTO-DA-FE

Solemn ritualistic burning of Jews and other "heretics" at the behest of the inquisitional authorities of the Catholic Church. "Trials" were conducted in the presence of the clergy and invariably ended in confession under torture by fire, skinning alive, bone-crushing, etc. The verdict was almost always: burn them alive.

AVIGNON, COUNCIL OF

Proposed cessation of all intercourse between Christians and Jews (1567). It forbade Christians to employ Jewish physicians, to enter Jewish homes, to participate in Jewish festivals, to seek employment by Jews, or to serve as their masons or barbers. The Jews were rigidly confined to ghettos.

In 1616 the Pope expelled the Jews altogether from Avignon. Prior to their expulsion a number of Jewish children were secretly baptized by Dominican monks and so lost to their parents.

AVILA

In this Spanish town near Madrid in 1491 a child from "La Guardia," a village that never existed, was allegedly found dead. A Jewish shoemaker, his brothers and father

12

were accused by the Church of having killed the child (later canonized) and drinking its blood for Passover. The accused admitted, under torture, all points of the indictment. Following their burning, all Jews in this little town were murdered and their homes sacked. The Catholic clergy appropriated the synagogue for a church.

AVITUS, SAINT

This bishop of Clermont, France, in 576 gave the Jews in his diocese the choice of baptism or exile. The synagogue was burned.

B

BABI YAR

Ravine near Kiev. Here, in the Second World War, German *Einsatztruppen* shot and killed over forty thousand Jewish civilians, mostly women and children.

The Ukrainian population, its anti-Semitism long nurtured by the clergy, used the place of mass burial as a dumping ground. World pressure is being exerted on the Ukrainian authorities to erect a memorial to the victims.

Kiev remains today a center of anti-Semitic activity in the Ukraine, and its Academy of Sciences has repeatedly published tracts against the Jewish religion and ideology.

BAKUNIN, MICHAEL (1814-1874)

Offspring of wealthy Russian aristocracy, he was raised in the "Zid" (Jew) hating atmosphere of a Czarist Greek Orthodox parochial school and an officers' training center.

Intrigued by anarchistic ideas, he left the service and spent his time as a semi-journalistic do-nothing. A colorful demagogue and pamphleteer, he fell out with socialists of all denominations. However, one thing the Christian socialists and Communists had in common was hate for the Jew, which they had acquired with their earliest reading and listening.

Proudhon, like his deadly adversary Marx, accused the Jews of being capitalistic parasites, refusing to work and aiming to conquer the Christian world through Jewish capitalism. The Jews, he claimed, killed the first socialist, Jesus Christ, and will continue to do likewise. However, claimed Bakunin, Jewish socialists and Communists were actually crypto-capitalists who worked hand in hand for a Jewish victory. In fact, Bakunin wrote, Marx and Rothschild were two of a kind.

It is remarkable how close this type of "thinking" comes to that of Bakunin's contemporary, the French Catholic leader, Drumont, who like Hitler, later charged Jews with being both ultra-capitalist and ultra-Communist.

Credo quia absurdum.

BARCELONA

In this capital of Catalonia took place the public dialogue between Moses Ben Nachman and Pablo Christiani in 1263. Dominican friars, who later took a bloody hand in the Grand Inquisition, compelled the Jews to listen to their conversion sermons. The priesthood, as it gained power, pressed for laws restricting the Jews. A Jew or Jewess meeting a priest had to kneel down in the street.

In 1391, while the massacre of Jews at Palma on the island of Majorca was still going on, bands of Church-incited marauders stormed the Barcelona ghetto in a rampage of slaughter and plunder. Most Jews died defending their families; a few converted to the loving Church.

Barcelona was *"Judenrein."*

BARRIOS

Spanish equivalent of "concentration camps," established during the fourteenth and fifteenth centuries by order of the Catholic authorities for Jews and Semitic Christians (Marranos). By decree of the Cortes of Toledo (1480), all Jews who had not fled the barrios in the city were to be burned later.

The barrios of Toledo were similar to the "model" ghetto of Theresienstadt established in Czechoslovakia under Hitler, in that Jews were given a certain amount of self-government. The outcome in both enclosures was identical.

BASEL

In this Swiss canton the populace was subjected to anti-Semitic sermons late into the nineteenth century. In 1839 Basel expelled all Jews. On November 17, 1857, a law was passed forbidding Jews to settle, trade or ply a craft.

For the Medieval roots of Basel's Jew hatred, see *Black Death*.

BASKET TAX

The right to collect this tax on Kosher meat, trade licenses and traditional Jewish wearing apparel was leased to the highest bidder by Czarist Russia. It is a carryover from a privilege granted to Catholic monasteries. Even on skullcaps and the wigs prescribed for women they levied a burdensome taxation. In Russia the tax was first decreed on December 31, 1844, and remained in force until the twentieth century.

BAUER, BRUNO (1809-1882)

Influential Protestant theologian in Germany who sermonized persuasively that the oppression of Jews by Christians was justified, they being the killers of God. Also, that the Jews had never contributed anything to civilization, unlike the Germans, who were the essence of mankind.

BAVARIA

In this German state, the birthplace of Nazism, few Jews remained after the expulsion ordered by the Elector Max Emanuel on March 12, 1715. It was a pitiful few, their ancestors having been put to death on flimsy Church-inspired accusations of host-nailing, blood-drinking, well-poisoning, plague-creating, crucifixion-defiling, etc.

Burned in Munich, in 1285, were 180 Jews for allegedly having bled to death a Christian child in the synagogue. In 1298 a priest was responsible for spreading the rumor that Jews were driving nails through holy wafers, thereby crucifying Christ again. Among those murdered that year because of a maddened cleric were 628 Jews in Nuremberg (Mordecai ben Hillel, the famous scholar, was one of the victims).

In Deggendorf, in 1337, the whole Jewish population was butchered because a Jew supposedly broke a holy wafer. A memorial chapel was erected on the spot of the butchery and pilgrimages were arranged by the Catholic Church which still go on.

Ten years after the Deggendorf "purification" the Bavarians, driven by their priests, fell upon more than eighty Jewish communities in their land with pitchfork and sickle and killed every man, woman and child. Ten thousand fell, victims of this latest, the "Black Death," accusation.

Numerous chapels and churches still stand in the heartland of Hitlerism, erected in commemoration of the "cleansing." These churches were consecrated to Mary, holy mother of Christ. It is quite likely that among the ten thousand Jews murdered then—as among the six million murdered later—there were direct relatives and descendants of the Jewish gentlewoman and her Hebrew spouse Joseph.

BELGIUM

As late as 1898 a solemn procession of Belgian clergymen paraded through the streets to commemorate a bloody and torture-ridden trial of 1370 for "desecration of the Host."

The Church has a long and vindictive memory. In 1370 someone imagined he saw a Jew break a wafer, and a hundred of Christ's kinsmen, children among them, were roasted like chickens—only no one roasts a chicken live, and even cannibals kill their victims by knife, not by slow fire.

*

Gauthier de Castillon (c. 1160), provost of the Chapter of Tournai, distributed a three-volume set of calumnies against the "Christ killers" that deepened and spread anti-Semitism throughout all churches of the land.

*

In 1261, Alix of Brabant, widow of Henry III, inquired of Thomas Aquinas, the renowned doctor of philosophy if she could—without harming her Christian conscience!—deprive her subject Jews of their funds. The sage Dominican in a brilliant piece of casuistry reassured her that she could, provided she left the God killers enough to carry on.

What price scholasticism?

*

In 1370, "five hundred Jews were dragged through the streets of Brussels and without distinction of sex or age mutilated until dead." Eighteen tableaux showing Jews driving nails through holy wafers and blood flowing from the host were painted in the cathedral and can still be seen.

BELLOC, HILAIRE (1870-1953)

Most articulate spokesman of English Catholicism, propagated the idea that the Jews pursue only one object: money. The Jews have no true interest in science, philosophy or the arts; they look only for material gain.

Goebbels frequently took a leaf from his writings. Along with Chesterton, Belloc was repeatedly honored by the Catholic Church.

BENEDICT VIII (1012-1024)

On Good Friday of 1021 an earthquake followed by a hurricane occurred in Rome, creating havoc in the city. The Pope arrested a number of Jews, who allegedly had put a nail through a holy wafer the day before, as the probable cause of God's wrath. They all confessed and were burned.

Good Friday is a bad day in the Jewish calendar and Holy Week the terror of the year. Religious persecution of the Jews rises to its peak at these times.

BENEDICT XIII

This schismatic Pope in 1415 prohibited the "existence" of the Talmud and prescribed that every Jew attend official Church sermons under penalty of death.

BENEDICT XIV (1675-1758)

One of the monsters to wear the Tiara. In 1747 he issued a bull that all Jewish children over seven years of age could be baptized, even against the will of their parents.

He also reactivated the law of 1732 which prohibited Jews from spending even a single night outside the ghetto.

The year 1732 was the birth-year of George Washington.

BERNANOS, GEORGES (1888-1948)

Dominant French Catholic writer, "obligatory" author in French high schools and colleges. This gentle "friend of every priest" wrote "When the right moment comes, clean out the Jews, the way a surgeon removes an abscess."

I suppose Hitler and Eichmann should be named "Surgeons of the Century."

BERNARD OF CLAIRVAUX, SAINT (1090-1153)

Founder and abbot of a Cistercian monastery, adviser to popes, author of books on "Humility," "Love of God," "Grace," "Charity," etc.

Of the Jews the saintly philosopher said: They are no better than beasts, in fact "More than bestial . . . They are of the Devil."

Julius Streicher urged the killing of all Jews as the "offspring of the Devil."

BERNARDINUS OF FELTRE (1439-1494)

Fanatical Franciscan friar who traveled through Italy, as a self-appointed protector of Christian children "whom the Jews want to steal and crucify." He had a strong appeal to the devout masses of Italian serfs and servants, who were incited to bloody riots along the trail of the mad Franciscan, especially during Holy Week.

For a donation, the poor and ignorant got a drop of "Holy Water" from the priest to cleanse their shabby homes of Jews and devils. The friar depicted all Jews as moneybags who exploited the Christian masses—another of the saintly predecessors of Hitler.

BERTHOLD, BISHOP OF STRASBOURG

Presided at a meeting of the Council of Towns of Alsace, held in 1348 amid the wave of Black Death accusations against the Jews. The learned Bishop demanded that all Jews be exterminated *"Mit Kind und Kegel"* ("bag and baggage"—literally, "with child and brat"), an expression that Hitler later adopted.

BEZIERS

In this French town it was the custom for many hundreds of years during the Middle Ages to stone Jewish

19

homes on Good Friday, when the death of Jesus was commemorated. Good Friday and Palm Sunday sermons throughout the Christian world have given the cue to attack or insult Jews as killers of God.

BIROBIDZHAN

A Siberian ghetto colony established by Joseph Stalin in 1934, the year of the great anti-Semitic purge, so that the Jewish people of the Soviet Union could be shipped off into permanent isolation. Stalin was well acquainted with the papal as well as Lutheran utopian projects for permanent segregation of the Jews.

The Birobidzhan plan failed because the Stalin government was unable at that time to spare the Jewish scientists, administrators and professional personnel needed by a Russia engaged in crash industrialization. However, Stalin's youthful orthodoxy in religion prevailed and he vent his anti-Semitism, like the earlier Orthodox leaders of Russia, in systematic police pogroms against the Jews. Over fifty thousand "expendable" Jewish writers, artists, teachers and political figures were executed, while Russian Orthodox priests scraped favor with their Communist masters by preaching against the Jewish menace and all "internationalists."

The Hitler war interrupted the anti-Jewish measures, which were taken up by Stalin again, as soon as peace was assured. This time the Jews were assailed with the age-old Christian accusation of being engaged in an international conspiracy to conquer the world (the New York-Tel Aviv Axis). Ancient statements by early Christian Church Fathers (Chrysostom, Eusebius, Justin) were dug up to support the contention that the Jews were using the synagogues to smuggle currency (moneychangers of the Gospel) and, in general, to plot evil against their neighbors.

The Judas people were hiding enemy silver (American) in their Torahs and prayer shawls. Indeed, Stalin's propagandists only repeated the priest-inspired charges of Constantine, that the synagogues were places of ill repute.

During the Stalin era, Jew hate rose to high pitch. Hundreds of Jews were shot for "economic" offenses in widely publicized "trials," in which great emphasis was placed on the "Jewish origin" of the accused. Torahs, Talmuds, prayer shawls, even Yarmulkas were offered in "evidence" to show where Jews were hiding American money.

In Russia's satellites, Jewish officials from ministers on down were executed as Judases. Slansky in Prague and Anna Pauker in Bucharest were only two of those singled out for inquisition treatment as enemy Jews.

In 1953, the inquisition terror culminated in the "Jewish Doctor Accusation." Following closely the Catholic and Orthodox admonition to Christians that Jewish physicians always plan to kill Christians, Stalin accused his own Jewish doctors of just such deviltry. Anti-Semitism flared higher and higher. Telegrams poured in from the Orthodox Patriarch and priests alike demanding immediate execution of the Jew doctors.

Only Stalin's death prevented a repetition of a German-style massacre of the Hebrew people in the Soviet Union. The Tiflis seminary student joined his fellow priests of anti-Semitic persuasion wherever such men go, and he left a heritage of revived Jew hate that will take generations to obliterate.

BLACK DEATH

On January 9, 1349, all the apprehended Jews of the Swiss city of Basel were burned by a mob, infuriated by Church sermons which accused the Jews of deliberately giving the current plague, known as the Black Death, to Christians. The Jewish cemetery was destroyed—the burned require no burial—and the old tombstones with their Hebrew inscriptions used for the building of fortifications.

Again the Catholic Church preceded the Nazi Germans

21

in blasphemy. The Church killed Jews without giving them even the dignity of burial and consigned consecrated tombstones to war use. The clergy transformed the synagogue into a church.

It was only in 1869 that Jews were readmitted to Basel. The poison of Jew hatred lingers on.

BLOOD DRINKING, RITUAL. See Vampires.

BLOOD PURITY

with the Germanic strain, of course, representing the pure and the Semitic the corrupting element, was most successfully promulgated by the untutored Austrian, Adolf Hitler; the Führer sent out a "welcome-wagon" of florid racial propaganda, and thousands of German philosophers and theologians jumped on it to create a new anthropology, with the Jew next to the gorilla and the Teuton next to Christ.

All this was hardly new. Rampaging Castilian priests of the fifteenth century denied even the dubious sanctuary of Christianity to the desperate Jews of Inquisition Spain because of their impure Semitic blood. (Question: Was Christ of Iberian or Teutonic blood?) Hitler's clamor for "purity of blood" was only an echo of inflamed Spanish Catholicism which used the identical phrase. See *Limpieza de sangre.*

BLOY, LEON (1846-1917)

Leading French Catholic author, who wrote of the Jews: "It is impossible to earn the esteem of a dog if one does not feel an instinctive disgust for the synagogue." Further: To love Jews is a suggestion at which "nature revolts." Bloy's works are standard texts in all French high schools and liberal arts colleges.

BOOK BURNING

was another one of the ways in which the Christian churches expressed their hate of Judaism. We find it throughout the history of Christianity. As late as 1731, the Dominican Giovanni Antonio Costanzi instigated a drive to collect and burn all "Jewish" literature.

In September of 1553 all Hebrew books in the city of Bologna, Italy, were burned at the behest of Pope Julius III. He was only one of many book burners in the Vatican.

Despite their theological differences, on the point of anti-Semitism and especially the burning of Jewish literature Protestants and Catholics were hand in hand then, and for hundreds of years later.

In 1753 Pope Benedict XIV renewed the search in the ghettos of the Papal States. The notorious book burnings by Goebbels were only one of the many "mild" forms of anti-Semitism for which the Christian churches supplied a historic precedent.

BORION

in North Africa; it was, in 535, the site of concentrated clerical anti-Semitism. All synagogues were closed and Jewish religious practices, such as Matzoh eating, circumcision, bar mitzvah, marriage and burial rites, were outlawed.

BOSSUET, JACQUES BENIGNE (1861-1925)

This benign church leader of seventeenth-century France, appealing to both Catholics and Protestants, sermonized: "The Jews are monsters, hated universally. They are beggars and the butt of the world's jokes. Thus has the Lord punished them for killing His Son."

Such sentiments are typical of church preaching in this era.

BRESLAU

was the scene, together with Erfurt and Mainz, of large-scale extermination of Jews in the fourteenth century. Plague-ridden Germans took their vengeance on the Christ killers.

BROGLIE, VICTOR-CLAUDE (1757-1794)

President of the French Revolutionary Assembly, this representative of a princely Catholic family led the opposition against emancipation of the Jews. He was defeated.

BROWN CARDINAL

On March 9, 1939, Cardinal Theodor Innitzer was summoned to Rome by Pope Pius XII, together with the three German Cardinals: Adolf Bertram, Michael von Faulhaber and Karl Josef Schulte. After his reign of only one week the former German Nuncio, Pacelli, decided to send a lengthy handwritten letter of well-wishing to German Chancellor Hitler, who by then had already put underground thousands of Jewish children and hapless civilians, had burned all synagogues, etc., etc.

The good Pope had already sent through his office the usual perfunctory well-wishing messages to all other heads of state; with Hitler he felt compelled to communicate by his personal pen.

Cardinal Innitzer at this historic meeting suggested that His Holiness address the Führer with the respectful "Thou" (*Sie*). He emphasized that in the spirit of the Pacelli-Hitler Concordat of 1933, all teaching priests no longer greeted their pupils with the ancient "Praised be Jesus Christ" but with the new "Heil Hitler, praised be Jesus Christ."

Cardinal Faulhaber of Munich had already in March of 1934 greeted the Nazi Minister of the Interior, Adolf

Wagner, with "Heil Hitler" and Cardinal Innitzer regularly signed his name with "Heil Hitler."

On March 18, 1938, the month of the annexation of Austria by Hitler, which the Cardinal strongly supported, he wrote to the Gauleiter of Vienna, Josef Bürckel: "I enclose a declaration of loyalty by our Bishop, from which you can take that we Bishops *voluntarily and without duress* have fulfilled our duty. Thus our declaration will follow fine mutual cooperation."

And indeed the Cardinal and the Gauleiter worked hand in glove until the very end of the Austrian regime.

On March 15, 1938, two days after Hitler's arrival in Vienna at the head of the Nazi troops, Cardinal Innitzer met Hitler in a special audience in the Hotel Imperial and assured the Führer of the loyalty of his church. This is the day when Hitler spoke dreamingly of a "Religious Spring" in Germany.

On March 27 the Cardinal composed a pastoral letter, the text of which was first sent to the Gauleiter for approval and signed by Innitzer "with special assurance of esteem and Heil Hitler."

This document, oozing with subservience and Hitler adulation, was read from the pulpits of all Austrian Catholic churches on the last Sunday of March, 1938.

As a postscript Innitzer added that the struggle of Hitler is "visibly a subject of the blessings of divine providence."

On March 31, 1938, Innitzer wrote to the Gauleiter Bürckel: "I wish to emphasize that the support of the Hitler plebiscite by our Bishops is principally to be considered as the voice of our common German confession."

Like his Pope, Cardinal Innitzer uttered not a single word of protest when a quarter of a million Viennese Jews were shipped to fearful forms of execution.

BRUNNER, SEBASTIAN (1814-1893)

A Catholic priest and journalist who published violent anti-Semitic attacks in Vienna. His personal journal, *Wiener Katholische Kirchenzeitung,* was finally silenced by court action. At the sensational trial in Vienna it came to light that his anti-Semitica were largely plagiarized from older sources. His whole campaign was revealed to have only one purpose: money, gained by the time-worn technique of publishing scandalous material to increase circulation. Father Brunner was a precursor of Julius Streicher.

BRUNO, GIORDANO (1548-1600)

Eristic member of the Dominican order, who referred in his *Spaccio* to the Jews as a mangy and leprous people who "deserve to be exterminated."

This Catholic nonconformist, himself in later life a victim of prejudice, wished of the Jews that their offspring might be exterminated before birth!

One of the many steps of Christian theologians toward *Die Endlösung* of the Jewish "question."

BRUNSWICK

and other German provinces suffered severe anti-Semitic riots in 1540 in response to the hate polemics of Martin Luther. The Jews' position remained barely tolerable until the Napoleonic era.

BUCHAREST

In 1801 the Orthodox populace of this Rumanian city fell upon the Jews, who were accused of ritual blood drinking by the Orthodox clergy. This charge had been made against the Jews almost fifteen hundred years before by the favorite saint of the Orthodox, Chrysostom. One hundred twenty-eight Jews had their throats cut.

BUERGER

Hitler's edict depriving the Jews of all citizen's rights is only an emulation of a similar order issued under heavy Catholic pressure by the Stadtrat of Frankfurt, a/M. in 1480. Jews who, by direct command of Pope Pius II (1458-1464), had been restricted to a ghetto in Frankfurt, were referred to as *Hundejuden* (dog Jews) in all city records since 1460.

BURNING OF SYNAGOGUES

A feature of the infamous *Kristallnacht* in Germany of a generation ago, it was widely practiced in the years of the early Church Fathers: In Cortona, Italy, the local bishop incited the mob to arson and built a church in the synagogue's place. At Portus Magonis on the island of Minorca; at Tipasa in Africa, synagogues were burned and destroyed. Burning and savage attacks went on throughout the empire. When Theodosius II (408-450) wished to restore the synagogues, he was severely criticized by Simon Stylites (Saint!).

C

CANTERBURY, ARCHBISHOP OF

Closed all synagogues in his diocese in 1282. Under pressure from the Archbishop in 1290, all Jews still in England were expelled by King Edward I, with the Crown expropriating the property of the exiled. Seventeen thousand, the last Jews of medieval England, left for France and Belgium; many of them, however, never reached the shores of Europe, being thrown into the sea by avaricious ship captains.

CANTONISTS

Jewish boys in Czarist Russia who at the age of twelve were forcibly taken from their parents and forced into army service for twenty-five years. During these years they were subjected to weekly conversion lectures by Orthodox priests and monks and invariably "converted" to the Christian faith. Statements by such converts were employed in the Beiliss ritual trial case (1911).

CAPISTRANO, SAINT JOHN (1386-1456)

Fifteenth-century Franciscan propagator of the faith, papal appointee to head the Inquisition in northern countries, nicknamed "Scourge of the Jews," he ordained: "To fight the Jew is a duty of the Catholic, not a choice."

Many of Capistrano's malevolent practices were repeated by the twentieth-century propagators of Christian faith, such as Himmler, Frank and Eichmann. Hitler paraphrased the papal messenger of death by saying: "I am acting in accordance with God's Will by defending myself against the Jews; indeed, I am doing the Lord's work."

CARIDAD

A fifteenth-century Spanish religious association organized by the Bishop of Cordova that excluded all Marranos and other racially Semitic Christians from membership. As in Hitler Germany many of the Catholics of Semitic origin were finally put to a cruel death by the roving mobs of the bishop.

CARNIVAL

A pre-Lent period of public amusement in Rome established by Pope Paul II, in which the local Jews were made to play contemptuous parts, ending in injury or death.

28

The church-incited riffraff of Rome prevented the Jews from ending their forced run, and otherwise assaulted and molested them.

Not until January 28, 1668, was there an end made to this "sport." Instead, the papal authorities accepted a yearly "tax" of 300 scudi which was extorted from the Jewish population up to the accession of Pius IX in 1846.

Even the delivery of the extortion money was accompanied by abuse, kicking and slander of the Jewish delegates.

CASA SANTA

The "Holy House," reserved for the examination of men and women suspected of heresy by the Dominican friars of the Inquisition. In Spain their favorite "guests" were Jews who had converted to Christianity and their descendants.

Many of the instruments of "investigation" to be found in the *Casa Santa* were copied to a nail by the Gestapo for their latter-day headquarters.

CATECHESE CHRETIENNE ET LE PEUPLE DE LA BIBLE, LA

A basic work by the French priest Paul Démann, examining a great number of French-language religious texts used in France, Belgium, Switzerland and Canada. Here is how some of the parochial school books tell the Gospel stories:

"The crowd followed Jesus, the majority were Jews, His enemies [!], who wished to see Him die."

"Now those evil [!] men, they were Jews [!], spoke."

"But the [!] Jews were heartless [!] and yelled, Crucify Jesus!"

"The heart of the [!] Jews was as stone."

"The wicked [!] Jews took delight in watching Christ's suffering."

The above are verbatim quotations appearing in the survey of catechisms by the distinguished French theologian, Father Démann.

It is not surprising that graduates of such religious schools welcomed Hitler's arrival in France with satisfaction rather than dismay, and that a great number of French priests cheerfully fell in with the anti-Semitic program of the Nazi-Vichy government.

CATECHISM

"Sidic" a new ecumenical journal edited in Rome by Catholic clergymen, published in its June, 1967, issue a series of critical reports on the distorted picture of the Jew drawn in Catholic catechisms. Current German and Spanish texts continue to send seeds of "gospel-anti-Semitism" through its liturgical literature.

CATECHISMS

and other liturgical manuals of the Church are characteristically interspersed with anti-Semitism.

The celebrated catechism of Abbé André Hercule de Fleury (1653-1743), which in two centuries went through 172 editions, reads: "Did Jesus have enemies?—Yes, the carnal Jews.—To what point did the hatred of Jesus' enemies go?—To the point of causing his death.—Who was it who promised to hand him over?—Judas Iscariot.—Why was this city [Jerusalem] treated in this way [destroyed]? —For having caused the death of Jesus.—What became of the Jews?—They were reduced to servitude and scattered throughout the world.—What has become of them since?— They are still in the same state.—For how long?—For seventeen hundred years."

Such lessons were read to millions of children all over the Catholic world *and still are being read with hardly any change.*

Here is a section from the catechism of Gambart, written especially for the uneducated:

"Some insulted him; others, with the backs of their hands, struck his noble and gentle mouth; others spat into his face (for it was the custom of the Jews to spit into the faces of those whom they cast out from among themselves) ; others tore out his beard or pulled at his hair, and thus trampled under their accursed feet the Lord of the angels. . . . And still spitting into his noble countenance, they struck his head with a stick, so that the thorns of his crown sank into his head and made the blood flow down his cheeks and over his forehead. . . . Pilate commanded that in this shameful and inhuman state he be led before all the Jewish people, who had remained outside in order not to sully themselves on the day of the Sabbath. But these accursed sons of the Devil all cried out with one voice: Take him away, take him away, crucify him."

Is it surprising that our people consider the Christian Sunday schools and seminaries no better than schools of defamation of the Jewish race, that we are convinced that the disdain for Jews taught in the churches to the young will remain with them emotionally no matter what manner of rationalization is offered them in later years? Theories acquired in formative years can be corrected, but prejudices and hates not so readily. The horror stories about the Jews remain in the hearts of Christians who have long given up the faith and teachings of the Church. That is why the better among them, who would not hurt a living creature, could watch with equanimity while tortures and death were perpetrated on Jews.

The hate mythology of the Gospel and the catechism makes it impossible for the Jews to be accepted by their Christian neighbors as mere people. In the soul of almost every Christian there lies a deep-set repugnance for the killer of God, a traumatic instillation of his youth. Indeed, he may no longer remember that it was in the church edifice that he acquired the *bacillus anti-Semiticus*.

The catechetical disease remains endemic, according to *Sidic*, a journal devoted to reform of Christian-Jewish relations which is published by the Catholic Sisters of Sion in

31

Rome. While "very good beginnings" are noted in the elimination of anti-Semitic references from catechisms in France, the United States, and some other countries, *Sidic* finds little comparable effort in Italy and complains that "seeds of Christian-type anti-Semitism" are to be found in current German texts. The journal's chief editor has been quoted as saying: "The Christian problem is to change a whole mentality, and this will take a lot of hard work."

CATHERINE I (1684-1727)

Devout Czarina of Russia who, upon the direct request of the Ukrainian clergy, expelled all Jews from their territory (1727).

CATHOLIC SCHOOLS

According to a report published in 1966 under the title *Catholic Schools in Action* (Notre Dame University), Catholic schools in America produce in 53 per cent of the students an unfavorable image of the Jew. The same report shows that only 33 per cent manifest a bias against the Negro.

CENTINELA CONTRA JUDIOS

Collection of Spanish tales published in 1728, which resurrected vicious fables about the Jews—among them one referring to "Jews that were born with worms in their mouth, descendants from a Jewess who ordered the crucifixion blacksmith to make the nails blunt."

CHAMBERLAIN, HOUSTON STEWART (1855-1927)

Son-in-law of the vitriolic anti-Semite Richard Wagner, authored *Foundations of the Nineteenth Century,* a racist volume that became the bible of German "anthropologists" in the thirties. By claiming superiority of the Teutons over all other people, Chamberlain's book flattered the strident inferiority complexes of the Hitler era. Julius Streicher published sections of it (illustrated) in his *Der Stürmer*. He called it the greatest book since the Gospels.

CHAMBRES ARDENTES

The "burning rooms" of France in which converted Jews, accused of "back-sliding" by the Catholic clergy, were put to death. Inquisition trials continued in France up to 1772.

CHAUCER, GEOFFREY (1340-1400)

Author of *The Canterbury Tales*, in which he recites the ritual murder story of a sweet-singing little Christian lad, set upon by evil Jews, who slit the child's throat and then throw the body into the privy pit.

"The Prioress's Tale" is an early example of Jew hate, spread originally by the English Church Schools, which has become embedded in classic literature to influence one generation after another of secular readers. Its author was the first of English literature's anti-Semitic three—the second, William Shakespeare, propagandized the Jew as a malevolent usurer in his *Merchant of Venice*, while the third, Marlowe, defamed a Jew as a well poisoner in his *Jew of Malta*.

Here are some of Chaucer's loathsomely sweet verses which perpetuate the infamy heaped on the hapless Jews of England:

In Asia once there was a christian town
In which, long since, a Ghetto used to be
Where there were Jews, supported by the Crown
For the foul lucre of their usury,
Hateful to Christ and all his company. . . .
As I have said, this child would go along
The Jewish street and, of his own accord,

33

Daily and merrily he sang his song
O Alma Redemptoris. . . .
First of our foes, the Serpent Satan shook
Those Jewish hearts that are his waspish nest,
Swelled up and said, 'O Hebrew people, look!
Is this not something that should be redressed?
Is such a boy to roam as he thinks best
Singing, to spite you, canticles and saws
Against the reverence of your holy laws?'
From that time forward all these Jews conspired
To chase this innocent child from the earth's face.
Down a dark alley-way they found and hired
A murderer who owned that secret place;
And as the boy passed at his happy pace
This cursed Jew grabbed and held him, slit
His little throat and cast him in a pit.
Cast him, I say, into a privy-drain,
Where they were wont to void their excrement.
O cursed folk of Herod come again,
Of what avail your villainous intent?
Murder will out, and nothing can prevent
God's honour spreading, even from such seed;
The blood cries out upon your cursed deed. . . .
The Provost, praising Christ our heavenly king
And His dear mother, honour of mankind,
Bade all the Jews be fettered and confined. . . .
The Provost then did judgement on the men
Who did the murder, and he bid them serve
A shameful death in torment there and then
On all those guilty Jews; he did not swerve.
'Evils shall meet the evils they deserve.'
And he condemned them to be drawn apart
By horses. Then he hanged them from a cart.

CHESTERTON, G. K. (1874-1936)

Catholic writer, standard author in parochial schools of
today, expressed his regret that the Crusaders who slaugh-

tered Jewish men, women and children and then plundered their homes could not be canonized.

CHILE

The long arm of the Inquisition reached out from Rome and Madrid to the New World to arrest, torture and burn hundreds of Marranos, usually spotted and spied on by "familiars" of the Holy Office.

The records show only wealthy "offenders," which would seem to indicate that here, as in other places, the greed of the authorities was a larger motive than zeal against "heresy."

As late as 1852 the Jewish musician Michael Hauser escaped a "trial" only by flight. Anti-Semitism in Chile has never subsided. The churches keep it alive with fiery sermons.

CHMIELNICKI, BOGDAN ZINOVI (1595-1657)

Hetman of the Zaporogian Cossacks in the Ukraine; like Stalin, a devout student of the Greek Orthodox faith. It was not difficult for him to persuade his Cossack followers that the Jews, accursed by God, should be obliterated.

His butchery of the unarmed Jewish civilians in Poland and the Ukraine was so horrid as to forbid description. Europe was aghast at the atrocities perpetrated on hundreds of thousands of women and children.

In his early years Chmielnicki was a pupil of the Jesuits as well as Orthodox priests. He seems to have retained little from either denomination except fuming Jew hatred. His memory lives on in the Orthodox Church as a blessed defender of the faith.

In the Second World War the Germans were able to recruit from among the Ukrainians, perennially subject to anti-Semitic propaganda by the Greek Orthodox clergy, millions of Nazi collaborators and a whole army corps of volunteers for Hitler. The Ukraine is still the most anti-Semitic segment of the Soviet Union.

CHOSEN PEOPLE

The Ecumenical Council reiterated that the Chosen People were no longer the Jews but rather the faithful of the Catholic Church.

Unhappily, Julius Streicher, Hitler's man with the whip, had already lectured on this subject: "If somebody tells you the Jews were the Chosen People, don't believe him. Believe us instead. A chosen people does not practice ritual murder. You German youth must shout: 'We Germans hate the race which Jesus said came from the Devil.'"

The Gospel of St. John was correctly quoted: It says that the Jews were sons of the Devil.

Is it not time to clean up the book so the Streichers cannot use it?

CHRISTIAN ANTI-SEMITISM

There is none other. Political animosities in the present Arabic world are time-bound and ism-bound, like those among many other national or state groups. Pre-Christian quarrels of the Jews with Romans, Greeks, Egyptians, Persians or Syrians were local in time and place.

It is only the Christian religion as formulated in early Catholicism that has its very faith based on Jesus, the Son of God, and the Jew, Son of the Devil, the Killer of God. Christianity has anti-Semitism built in as part of its dogma.

Every one of the hundred references in the New Testament to the Jews is anti-Semitic. There is not one redeeming remark in the Christian Gospels concerning the Jew. The Jew is evil itself, killer of Christ, negator of Christianity, traitor to Christ, torturer of Christ, hater of all Christians.

The Gospels carry beautiful stories of Jesus filled with

36

excerpts from Hebrew wisdom literature. But in all these stories the Jew comes out the Devil. All the love in the book is reserved for the Gentiles; for the Jew, only contempt and a curse. The Jew is antichrist.

They want the Jew in the story. He makes it dramatic. Light against darkness. Good against Sin. God's Son against the Devil's Son. The Devil's Son is the Jew (John VIII:44). They need the Jew as the symbol of wickedness. They need anti-Semitism, it is the spice of their catechism.

Christian faith is not anti-Semitic; it is anti-Semitism itself.

And they will not erase it from their text no matter how much misery, suffering and death it may cause the living Jews. Because the living Jews are not their concern. They care only about the Jews of the Gospel; they need them as dramatis personae in their miracle play.

Singing hymns of mystic love, they step over the tortured bodies of ten million Jews whom their anti-Semitism had cut down or burned over the last two thousand years; just as the first Crusaders in the eleventh century drove the Jews of Jerusalem into their great synagogue, set the building afire and marched around the edifice chanting, "Christ, we adore Thee."

CHRISTIAN CAPITALISM

The nineteenth century saw Church anti-Semitism, nurtured for eighteen hundred years on the Gospels as expounded by the Church fathers, seek the new fields of social anti-Semitism. As socialism, Communism and even liberalism openly challenged Christianity, especially the Catholic Church, the priests and ministers naturally set their sights on these ideological rivals.

Instinctively they identified the new enemies with their old hate object, Judaism. Or perhaps their more astute publicists calculated that the Christian masses, imbued since childhood with the Gospel image of the Jew as a hateful

37

killer, would more readily reject Communism if it were depicted as a Jewish movement. Thus the Church could destroy two enemies with one blow.

Christian capitalism began its campaign in the late nineteenth century by stamping the Protestant convert, Karl Marx, as a Jew, although he himself was a most persistent and brazen anti-Semite. With the zeal characteristic of a convert, in his book, *The World Without Jews* (*Probleme zur Judenfrage*), Marx repeats every possible anti-Semitic shibboleth of the Catholic and Protestant churches, winding up with the hope for a world emancipated from Judaism.

Hitler, as he repeatedly insisted, continued the work of the Catholic Church by letting loose his propaganda against the "Jewish" Communists. The European Christians, especially the Germanic groups, succumbed to his Great Lies concerning the nefarious Jews. They copied old anti-Semitic principles and phraseology. The Jews were conspiring to destroy healthy Christian industry and individuality and replace it with a Jew-controlled Communist society; in this process they, the Jews, naturally would eliminate the Church and all Christian tradition.

Such grotesque accusations fell upon willing ears. For fifteen hundred years the Christians of Europe had been brainwashed—or shall I say brainsoiled?—by anti-Semitic demonology from pulpit and catechism. Now the gory oratory of Jew baiting came from the government itself, the new God. And the Church stood by smiling with sanctimonious satisfaction at the fresh outpouring of its old anti-Semitic hatred.

At this writing the churches have refused to absolve the Jew of God killing, refused to condemn anti-Semitism, refused to admit openly that the sermons were false, that the Jews are not arch-conspirators of Communism.

The Jews have no voice at all in the Red high command; none of the current strategists or theoreticians of the movement is of Jewish origin—yet Church papers continue to smear *the* Jew as the arch-Communist, just as they paint him as the arch-antichrist.

CHRISTIAN CONSCIENCE

occasionally comes to the fore, even in matters pertaining to Jews. In 1948 a Committee for Christian Aid to War Prisoners was formed in Germany, protesting vehemently the Allied war crime trials involving the top Nazi murderers.

Among the most active members and sponsors of said committee were Cardinal Josef Frings of Cologne, Catholic Bishop Johann Neuhäussler of Munich, Lutheran Bishop Theophil Wurm of Stuttgart and Lutheran Bishop Meiser of Munich.

These highly agitated clergymen, who watched the execution of Jewish families with admirable equanimity, could not rest in their efforts to set the Nazi killers free. They were supported by two religious organizations, the Roman Catholic *Caritas* and the Protestant *Evangelisches Hilfswerk*. The German weekly, *Christ und Welt*, led the campaign against Jewish "revenge" seekers.

Cardinal Frings and Bishop Wurm also headed the notorious "Committee for Justice" which became a rallying point for the former Nazi elite. Their Christian Aid Center in Munich supplied indicted Nazi executioners with material aid in escapes abroad and feverishly worked for reduction in sentences of Nazi criminals. Even Ilse Koch, "the Bitch of Buchenwald," she who decorated her lamps with shades made of Jewish skin, was released, though later re-arrested.

CHRISTIAN NAMES

were forbidden to Jews by many Catholic bishops and nobles. In fourteenth-century Spain the Cortes of Toro (1369) and of Burgos (1377) made this prohibition a point of Christian law. Here, too, Hitler revived an old Christian practice.

CHRISTIAN SERVANTS

were prohibited to the Jews by repeated bulls and papal orders. An archbishop in Sardinia, for example, ruled that offenders would be punished by receiving two hundred lashes. The Nazi Germans re-established the ban on employment of Christian servants by Jews.

CHRISTIAN TERMINOLOGY

was extensively used by the Nazi philosophers and political leaders, from Martin Heidegger to Alfred Rosenberg. In his eloquent encyclical *"Mit Brennender Sorge"* Pope Pius XI made reference to the many expressions taken from Christian theology by the Nazis.

Similar plagiarism is practiced by most anti-Semitic groups, who take advantage of latent as well as explicit anti-Semitism in Christian canon and liturgy simply by prefixing their movements with such adjectives as "Christian," "Crusader," "Evangelic," etc.

CHRISTIAN UNIVERSITIES

in Europe did not admit Jews to teaching positions until the late nineteenth century, in many instances not until the twentieth century. Throughout Catholic history Jewish students were handicapped in gaining admission or totally excluded. Hitler's expulsion of all Jews from the academic world, teachers as well as students, was only a variation of a thousand-year-old Catholic policy.

CHRISTIAN WOMEN

In reaction to the multiple suffering of the contemporary Hebrews: "They [the Jews] are receiving just what they measured out to Christians." (Protestant *Women's Voice*, March 26, 1953.)

Aren't these gentle Christian women like the nuns of Queen Isabella who carried faggots to the auto-da-fé? Such hostility makes it clear why Christian Europe watched indifferently the burning of the Jews.

CHRISTMAS

During Christmas of 1936 Julius Streicher in *Der Stürmer* called on "all German Christians" to cease doing business with "the killers of our dear Lord Christ."

"To be intimate with Jews is to defend the crucifiers of our Lord."

It almost reads like a quotation from the *Bullarium Romanum* of the Vatican.

At a Christmas celebration for school children the former school teacher, Julius Streicher, asked his audience: "Do you know who is the Devil?"

"The Jew, the Jew," came the response from the lips of all. Some of the older pupils even knew where the quotation came from: the eighth chapter of the Gospel of St. John.

The Church had done a great job of education on the Jewish problem.

Christmas still provides an opportunity to celebrate, not the Advent of Jesus, but *the* Jew as His Adversary.

In 1967 the vice-president of the school board of Wayne Township, New Jersey, issued a public statement urging voters to defeat two Jewish candidates for the board. Most Jews, he said, were liberals and likely to spend too much money on education. Then came the clincher:

"Two more votes and we lose what is left of Christ in our Christmas celebrations in our schools. Think of it."

In the subsequent election the two Jewish candidates were overwhelmingly defeated.

CHRYSOSTOM, SAINT JOHN (345-407)

Patriarch of Constantinople, by far the most influential preacher of his time, referred to in Catholic literature as "the bishop with the golden tongue." Here is some of his gilded rhetoric:

"The Jews are the most worthless of all men. They are lecherous, greedy, rapacious. They are perfidious murderers of Christ. They worship the devil, their religion is a sickness. The Jews are the odious assassins of Christ and for killing God there is no expiation possible, no indulgence or pardon. Christians may never cease vengeance, and the Jew must live in servitude forever. God always hated the Jews. It is incumbent upon all Christians [i.e., their duty] to hate the Jews."

Thus read the homilies of the foremost orator of early Catholicism.

CHUETA

Spanish corruption of *juéut,* diminutive form of the Catalonian word for "Jew"; name given to descendants of Catholic converts on the Spanish island of Majorca, who are still being ostracized by Gentile Catholics because they are of Jewish origin. See *Individuos de la Calle.*

CLEMENT, SAINT

Pope (88-97?), endeavored to blame the Jews for the Neronic persecution of the Christians. One of the earliest such innuendoes in Christian history.

CODEX THEODOSIANUS (438 A.D.)

This master compilation of Christian Romanism limited the Jews to private or secret religious observance. The Jews had become second-class citizens, to remain thus in most Christian lands until the great American and French revolutions. The Codex banned conversion to Judaism, while Catholic proselytism was encouraged. It permitted the conversion of Jewish children, whose parents could not disown them. A Jew was forbidden to acquire a Christian slave. (Similarly Hitler prohibited employment of Christian servants by Jews.)

CONCORDAT OF COLLABORATION

Nazi "legality" was immensely strengthened by the Concordat with the Vatican (July 20, 1933), an agreement which the Catholic Church had refused to grant the previous Weimar Republic. (Concordats did exist with such component German states as Bavaria, Prussia, and Baden.)

Hitler described the Concordat of Collaboration as an "unrestricted acceptance of National Socialism by the Vatican." Indeed it was, since it subordinated all cultural and educational activities of the Church to Nazi ideology and regimen. It began with the placing of Hitler's portrait on the walls of all Catholic parochial and Sunday schools—and ended with the church bells ringing at every Nazi victory, including the arrest and transportation of the last Jew from every town and hamlet in Germany.

The sellout of Catholicism to Hitler began not with the people but with the Vatican Curia. For Rome it was only a repetition of the Concordat it had previously made with Mussolini. The German bishops followed the Vatican, represented by its Secretary of State, Cardinal Pacelli, later Pius XII; the priests obeyed the Bishops, and the parishioners fell in line.

Never, after the signing of the Concordat, did the Church protest against Hitler or his barbarism; never against his satanic system of bloodshed, including the blood of a million Jewish children. When protests came they were invariably concerned with infractions against the interests of the Church. As Bishop Christoph Bernhard von Galen declared in 1935, "It is not my job to mourn past political structures or to criticize the present ones." Adolf Cardinal Bertram in

43

1936 most loyally declared: "Not a single pastoral letter of the German Catholic clergy ever criticized the National Socialist Movement or, God forbid, the *Führer*."

Pater Alfred Delp, one of the few exceptions to the closed ranks of subservient churchmen, bitterly warned before his execution (following the attempt against Hitler's life in July, 1944) : "The future historians of Germany will have to write the bitter chapter about the total failing of the Christian Churches."

CONFISCATION

The Grand Master of the Knights of the Hospital of Saint John in 1305 sent a memorandum to Pope Clement V, suggesting that half of the goods of the Jews be seized by the Church in punishment for Christ's killing. A similar suggestion had been made previously by another great crusading figure, Peter of Cluny.

The good Pope went further, much further, and had all Jews expelled from France, confiscating their goods.

Confiscation of Jewish property was the initial step in Hitler's internal policy, to be followed later by executions. By 1305 France had already had its Jew burnings; Pope Clement's expellees were only a remnant of the once considerable Jewish populace.

CONSTANCE

In 1349 monk-led Flagellants killed the "accursed" Jews of this Swiss town. The tombstones of their cemetery were used to build the great cathedral of the town.

Degrading restrictions burdened the few Jews who drifted back to Constance as late as the middle of the nineteenth century.

The use of consecrated Jewish tombstones as building material for new edifices and fortifications was widely practiced by the German Nazis as a sign of contempt for what

44

Bishop Luigi Carli, prominent in the Second Ecumenical Council, recently termed the "accursed Jewish religion."

CONSTANTINOPLE

Civil rights of Jews in this great city, which was once Byzantium, were severely curtailed from the time of the first Christian emperor, Constantine. Restrictions and humiliations imposed by the overbearing clergy of the Greek Church were incessant.

A new era came for the much harassed and persecuted Jews with the fall of Constantinople (1453) and extinction of the Byzantine Empire by Mohammed the Conqueror. The Moslems offered the Jews of the Renaissance sanctuary from certain destruction at the hands of the Christians of Western and Southern Europe.

Similarly, the position of the Jews in the Moorish segments of Spain was one of dignity and respect and stands in marked contrast to the vicious, bloody persecutions at the hands of the Catholic Church.

CONVERSION SERMONS

In 1577 Pope Gregory XIII (1572-1585) decreed that all Roman Jews, by pain of death, must listen attentively after their Sabbath services to a Catholic conversion sermon, first in the church San Benedetto alla Regola, later in Sant Angelo in Pescaria.

In 1823 Pope Leo XII re-established the ghetto in Rome, which had been rendered wide open by the victorious French troops of Napoleon; and he ordered the revival of forced conversion sermons on the Jewish Sabbath.

Not until the Garibaldi freedom uprising was the Papal yoke removed from the Jews in the Vatican state. On December 13, 1870, victorious King Victor Emanuel II granted the Jews all civic and political rights. After almost two thousand years the Jews of Rome were free of papal terror.

CORFU

On this Greek island in 1891 the local clergy of the Orthodox Church accused the Jews of having slain a child for its blood. Many Jews had to flee for their lives since the local authorities failed to protect them.

CORPUS JURIS CIVILIS (529-535)

Justinian's definitive Code of Roman law made the already draconic restrictions of the *Codex Theodosianus* still more rigorous. Christian theological considerations dominated all its "Jewish" legislation. Jews were not permitted to testify against a Christian, were barred from public functions, had only limited property rights, and their marriage to Christians was a capital offense. (Cf. the Nuremberg Laws.)

COUGHLIN, FATHER CHARLES EDWARD (1891—)

A blustering American version of the nineteenth-century German anti-Semitic court preacher Stöcker. In the 1930's, from his shrine of The Little Flower in Michigan, Father Coughlin used the new medium of radio to broadcast the same basic message to Depression-ridden America—"Blame the Jews!"—clothed in the same vague context of Christian Socialism. In case his listeners forgot the message, the "Radio Priest" repeated it in his own magazine, *Social Justice.*

In 1966, on the fiftieth anniversary in the priesthood of Father Coughlin, whose anti-Semitic radio chats bewildered America and gave aid and comfort to Hitler, the following eulogy was delivered to the ill-spoken priest:

"Father Coughlin was committed to a better social order, to a world of justice [!]—to a life worthy of man as a child of God—he was a giant in this generation."

Thus spake Mother Church about the man who, more than any other person on this continent, tried to justify

Hitler's persecutions of the Jews by smearing the victims with slanderous medieval charges.

COUNCIL OF BASEL (1431-1443)

Invoked by Pope Eugenius IV. Reinforced the familiar restrictions upon Jews—separate quarters from Christians, compulsory attendance at Church sermons, and prohibition of study at universities.

COUNCIL OF PARIS

forbade Christian midwives to attend Jewish women in labor (1212). Those who helped bring the brood of the Devil into this world would be expelled from the Holy Church.

CRETE

The Jews in medieval Crete were compelled by the Orthodox clergy to affix a wooden devil figure to their doors, to warn Christians against entering their homes.

CRUCIFIXION

The Roman leader Varus (139-169) crucified two thousand captive Jews within view of Jerusalem. The Romans were adept in crucifixion; it was their way. Crucifixion was never the Hebrew way. No criminal or rebel was ever crucified by Hebrews. Even the Jew-hating scribes of the Roman bishops blamed the Jews only for instigation, never crucifixion; and this to please their Roman benefactors beginning with Constantine—an opportunistic perversion of history to placate the powerful emperor.

CRUSADERS

on their first rampage took Jerusalem in 1099. The cross-emblazoned knights of Christian love herded all Jews into the great synagogue and burned them alive, man, woman and child. While the Temple was ablaze they marched around it singing, "Christ, we adore Thee." We even have drawings of this ceremony in contemporary diaries.

The Holy Sepulcher is a symbol that invokes religiosity in many Christians. To the Jews, however, it remains a fearful harbinger of bestial attacks on their people. Anti-Semitic fury preached in the Catholic churches by Crusading monks filled the rivers of France, Germany and Austria with the blood of Israel.

CUBA

The Inquisition was active in this island in the seventeenth and eighteenth centuries. In most cases the Holy Office put only wealthy Jews and Marranos to the torture. After they confessed and went to the pyre, their property was confiscated. Again, greed beclouds the religious issue.

It is reported that Spanish-language antisemitica finds a ready market among certain "right-wing" and "upper-class" Cuban emigrés in the United States. No matter what one's present troubles, it is comforting to blame the scapegoat learned about at mother's knee—Mother Church, that is.

CYPRIAN, SAINT

A third-century Bishop of Carthage, the most outstanding Catholic churchman of that era; demanded that all Jews be expelled at the point of the sword.

CYRIL OF ALEXANDRIA, SAINT (376-444)

This "Doctor of the Church" incited the Greek mobs to kill or expel the Jews (415). Not until the conquest of Egypt by the Moslems did a Jewish community come into its own again in Alexandria.

Cyril was a typical parchment theologian. He, like most

48

of the other Catholic Fathers, could not see a human soul for the black letter of his dogma. He looked at the massacre of Jews with equanimity; only texts could concern the saint.

CZERNOWITZ

In this Ukrainian town in 1579 the Jewish inhabitants were subjected to brutal and bloody outrage committed by the Voivode, Peter the Lame, a barbarian with two crucifixes on his chest, who proclaimed his determination to "avenge the killing of Christ."

D

DACHAU

On September 15, 1935, the notorious Nazi hate-sheet, *Der Stürmer*, printed a letter from a German girl, who wrote: "The Jew is speaking venomously against Christians; he should therefore be sent to Dachau." A similar reason was given by the Fourth Lateran Council for shutting the Jews up in ghettos.

DAGOBERT

This Frankish king (629-639) sent his royal edict to the Jews: convert or suffer expulsion. The Church was the rigorous host; the king was only the bouncer.

DAMASCUS INCIDENT

In 1840 a Franciscan friar disappeared in the city without trace. The Franciscan Order claimed that the Father was killed for his blood by Jewish Passover celebrants. Under torture, numerous Jews confessed, implicating others; some were executed, others finally released under pressure from humanitarian elements abroad.

DANZIG

In 1723 the Bishop of Danzig, failing to obtain an expulsion order against Jews from the city council, roused the mob against them. Most Jews were beaten to death; only a small number escaped.

DAUPHINE

In this old province of France in 1247 six Jews of Valréas were accused by Franciscan monks of having drunk the blood of a Christian child found dead. The Jews were horribly tortured, then burned. The Bishop of St. Paul-Trois-Châteaux thereupon imprisoned all Jews in his domain and robbed them of their properties.

DEGGENDORF

A Catholic tourist town in Bavaria whose great attraction is a Catholic church where sixteen oil paintings depict Jews in medieval dress desecrating wafers (hosts) with hammers, thorns and fire.

Ten thousand "worshipers" make the pilgrimage to Deggendorf yearly to absorb, along with the Mass, a booster shot of Jew hate.

The events which are commemorated by the Catholic clergy go back to September 30, 1337, when all the Jewish people of the town, including their children, were burned to death for cutting up consecrated wafers. Of course, the homes of the Jews were ransacked by the mob.

Today little Deggendorf still enjoys prosperity because of the armies of pilgrims who come, not to atone for the brutal massacre of innocent Jews, but to bewail the mutilated host.

To make the picture gallery understandable to the German pilgrims, the local padres adorned it with such explanations as: "The Holy Host is being scraped to the very blood by wicked Jews."

Only last year Bishop Rudolf Graber of Regensburg, responsible for Deggendorf, admonished its clergy not to deviate an iota from the "traditional practice."

Graber's General Vicar, Karl B. Hofmann, replied to critics: "We are not the only ones displaying such illustrations." Indeed, the Vicar is right.

Is it surprising that the Germans and Austrians found it easy to carry out Hitler's orders for Jew extermination? The Christian churches had readied twentieth-century Germans for their role in the holocaust.

DEICIDE

Introduced as a running theme of the Gospels to brand the Jew as a scapegoat for a Roman deed. Rome by then (fourth century) was the protector and benefactor of Christianity.

John Chrysostom (fourth century), the most influential Catholic theologian of all time, placed the "God killer" charge at the center of all Christian teachings. A millennium and more before Hitler he propagated an *identical* thesis: "The Jews are the pestilence of the universe."

The mainspring of anti-Semitism has remained, for 1500 years, the Christian accusation flung against the Jews of being the killers of Christ. Such accusation has not been withdrawn by the Vatican Council, but rather re-emphasized by the Schema that the Jewish leaders and the people who followed them pressed for the death of Christ.

Such teaching in all its gruesome detail of the piercing of hands and feet, the cruel demand of the Jews to break the bones of the dying Christ—all that remains and impresses itself indelibly upon the susceptible minds of Christian children.

When the Council, as a considerate afterthought, stated that the Jews of today are not responsible for this murder, and that even the Jews of antiquity were not *all* responsible —this is most generous!

However, the belated qualification has little effect upon

51

the boys and girls who for years are subjected to an obviously anti-Semitic and monstrous murder charge. I pray you, take a look at the Gospel of St. John, which is referred to as "the Spiritual Gospel." Of the 32 references to the Jews in this text, every single one is violently anti-Jewish.

As long as the charges that *the* Jews were the killers of the Christian God are not dropped—straight and unequivocally—the children raised in Christian Sunday schools will grow up in Jew hatred. I regret to say that the Schema of the recent Council, contrary to the wishes of Pope John XXIII—a truly great human being—is not the beginning of a new era in Catholic teaching, but rather a subtle confirmation of the old. Saying that my two-year-old grandson or the Jewish neighbor's wife across the street, is not a killer of Christ—well, no normal Catholic adult thinks differently. Here again we are given something by the Council that we have had for centuries. What we desire, and what all right-thinking people of the world desire, is that the Christian churches stop using the Jew as a scapegoat in their theological drama and once and forever drop the defamatory untruth of the Jews in particular being the killers of Christ.

One thing we know: those who followed Christ were all Jews. How many of those who urged His death were Greeks, Romans, Egyptians, Persians—no one knows. And everybody knows that the Procurator of Judea, Pontius Pilate, was a hard, all-powerful ruler, in behalf of the Roman Caesars, who reduced to ashes not only Alexandria, Athens, Carthage, Syracuse, Corinth, but eventually, Jerusalem. It suited the Bishops of Rome in the 4th century to make the Roman oppressor appear like a powerless, benevolent judge, totally subject to the whim and will of Jewish priests.

It is time that, in the spirit of Pope John XXIII, there be an end made to the deicide charge. There is no beginning or "initial stage" to withdrawing a false accusation. Justice knows only truth or falsehood; justice doesn't creep up on a judgment in multiple stages. The well-meaning people of the world are waiting for the Christian churches, not to make a beginning of justice, but to make an end to injustice.

And those who wait—after Vatican II, what did they hear?

"In conclusion, I hold it legitimate to be able to affirm that in the time of Jesus *all* the Jewish people were responsible *in solidum* for the crime of deicide, although only the leaders physically consummated the crime.

"It follows that Judaism must be considered as accursed by God." (*Pal. del Clero. XLIV,* April, 1966.)

Such an opinion, expressed by Bishop Luigi Carli, asserting perennial Jewish guilt for an alleged rabbinical judgment at a time when the majority of the Jews lived outside of the borders of Israel, reflects correctly the centuries-old attitude of anti-Semitic Catholicism.

What else could you call a religion that considers today's Jewish children (even new-born babies) *already* guilty of deicide and accursed by God? Only in German Nazism do we find a corresponding judgment of guilt. Hitler, too, theorized that he could gas to death Jewish infants because their grandfathers allegedly opposed Germany's expansionist war machine in World War I.

Catholicism of the Carli kind is kin to Hitlerism. Both condemn Jews, young or old, just because they are Jews, and both consider Jews *"vogelfrei,"* that is, without any legal protection. Of course, some Catholic liberals and pseudo-liberals are embarrassed by their own church's shameful history of anti-Semitic persecutions and are desperately trying to cover the gaping wounds left by the Carlifatti on the conscience of modern humanity.

Mankind has just done away with Hitlerism, without the help of the Christian ministers of Jesus, and now the Catholic Church would put the Jews right back where they were a generation ago, on the sacrificial block of bigotry.

Christian youth will continue to imbibe with their mother's milk Carli's interpretation of the Jew as a descendant of a Devil's brood who accomplished the death of Christ and whose religion is accursed by God forever.

The tragedy here is not just the opinion expressed in

53

official Catholic "learned" journals by a foxy old bishop with a decades-old background of Jew-baiting. The tragedy is that such a primitivist with his head on backward should be chosen by the Vatican to chair the Ecumenical Curia charged with the job of preparing a new "Declaration on the Jewish Question" that would take the Catholic Church out of the company of Himmler, Hitler and Eichmann and put Rome on the way to redemption and tolerance, as the late John XXIII planned, wished and inaugurated. What happened instead, through the Carlifatti, is that the Ecumenic message extolled by John XXIII died with the great Pontiff. What the world began to hear thereafter were no longer the celestial tones of peace and brotherhood, but the ugly mutters of a bedeviled Curia, taking up the old anti-Semitic chant: *Hep! Hep! Hep!*

We Jews have been betrayed by Vatican II. We have been betrayed by promises that were slowly, deliberately, twisted until we see through the final version of the Schema only the hooked cross of anti-Semitism.

DEMONS

The Jews are demons, proclaimed Pope Innocent III (1198-1217).

DEMONSTRATIO ADVERSUS JUDAEOS (160-235)

A brutal essay in which its author, Saint [*sic*] Hippolytus, "proves" that Jews must always be slaves because they "murdered" the only offspring of their Benefactor. He wishes for them most dire occurrences. Some later-day anti-Semites quote Hippolytus in defense of Nazism as an act of divine punishment upon the Jews.

DERROTA MUNDIAL

or *World Defeat,* a vicious "modern" anti-Semitic work in Spanish by Salvador Borrego, expounding the medieval

Catholic theorem of an international anti-Christian conspiracy by world Jewry.

DEVIL'S ADVOCATE

The Vatican's appointee to oppose beatification and canonization, the stages of raising to sainthood persons who may appear deserving of such recognition. I am not concerned here with errors of judgment in this intricate process of confirmation of holiness, such as elevation of nonexistent individuals or alleged victims of ritual murder who were presumptuously sanctified, as for instance little Simon of Trent.

I am touched by the endeavor to accord to the gentle Pope John XXIII public veneration, as I am shocked by the astonishing efforts of some reactionary Vatican circles to propose the author of the Nazi Concordat of Collaboration, Pope Pius XII, to such high status.

We Jews shudder at the word "saint," since so many of the vitriolic proponents of Jew slaughter, beginning with the early Church Fathers, were "saints." The Orders of Saint Dominic and Saint Francis provided the Inquisition with its bestial specialists for hundreds of years. The saintly friars conducted their interrogations and inevitable executions by tying Jewish men, women and children by their wrists to a stake or to a wall, at the foot of which slow fires burned to extend the agony of the victims.

Indeed, I know of no sainted, beatified or canonized figure in Catholicism that ever put a stop to the incessant War against the Jews. And if those pillars of the Church possess the power of heavenly intervention, God help us, in the light of their ominous darkness. I don't think that Saints who on earth led the war cry against us will be inclined to mercy above.

Will Pius XII now speak up in the heavens? He who stood silent on earth when the diabolical Hitler gassed the kin of Jesus?

DEVILS

In his pamphlet *Von den Juden und ihren Lügen,* Martin Luther declares that one may not mention the Jews in the same sentence with the Papists or even the Moslems, because the Jews were creatures of the Devil, as the Gospel teaches (John 8:44—"You are of your father, the devil.")

In numerous medieval church cartoons and illustrations the Devil carries a Jew-badge on his clothing.

Such barbaric anti-Semitic "religious" sentiment was prevalent, and most strongly so, in Germany, where Hitler found the ground well prepared for his "racial" campaign.

It was only a short step from the Gospel's "Devil Jews" to the Nazi story book quoted at the Nuremberg Trials:

> "The evil devil speaks to us
> Out of the Jewish face;
> The devil who in every land
> Is known as wicked plague."

DIALOGUE WITH TRYPHO

The first "objective" discussion by a Catholic theologian, Saint Justin Martyr (100-165), with an (imagined) rabbi, includes the Saint's opinion that all Jews are damned forever for having "murdered" the Lord.

DICTIONARIES

in Spanish and Portuguese countries still carry a number of objectionable Catholic Church definitions of "Jewish" terms. Jew is often defined as a synonym for "usurer," "swindler," "devil."

The new "revised" edition of the dictionary of the Portuguese language published by the Brazilian Literary Academy (Catholic directed) explains to its readers: "Synagogue: place for illegal business." This definition is remarkably close to Stalin's. Most Spanish and Portuguese and

56

many Italian "imprimatur" dictionaries are shot through with anti-Semitic didactics.

In this connection, it is worth noting a carry-over into a secular American work, Webster's International Dictionary (Third Edition). Among its definitions are: Jew (noun), "a person believed to drive a hard bargain"; Jew (verb), "to cheat by sharp business practice"; Jew down (verb), "to induce (a seller) by haggling to lower his price." The latter two definitions are accompanied by the explanation, "usually taken to be offensive."

None of these definitions were to be found in the previous Second Edition of Webster's. Their appearance now may be attributed to the editors' "pragmatic" approach to the American language, recognizing any and all words now in use, as they are used. Nonetheless, in this case such unqualified recognition serves to dignify and perpetuate the ancient stigma fastened by the Church on the People of the Book.

DIVINE(?) PUNISHMENT

The medieval Church, deep into modern times, was instrumental in depriving the Jew of civil rights, of his property, of his dignity and bodily safety.

The Church then turned around and proclaimed: "Mark the terrible fate of the Jew. This is divine punishment for his deicide! The wealth of the Church and the miserable conditions of the synagogue prove the guilt of the Jews."

DOGMA

If the whole of the four Gospels were to be accepted as absolute and genuine, then the statement of John, chapter 8, paragraph 44, that the (!) Jews were the offspring of the Devil is infallible.

Such an assertion implies that all the family of Jesus, all of them, and their children and their children's children, were the Devil's brood.

I cannot conceive a more monstrous assertion, a more insolent intolerance toward God's Chosen People and Christ's own kin than the above. No semanticism or word play can make this horrid insult to the Holy Family more palatable.

It is understandable why the Nazi hierarchy, from Hitler and Streicher down, quoted so frequently this sick verse of the Gospel of St. John. This gospel was promulgated under the aegis of Roman Bishops who were determined to make the Roman killers of Jesus look like angels and the Jews, who were the only ones whom He made His Apostles, into devils.

DOLLAR ANTI-SEMITES

appear sporadically in all Christian countries, even in the United States, which has an enviable record of fair play toward its Jewish citizens. Hate is a commodity. There always will be those willing to sell it in the manner of the patent medicine peddler. Their spiel, of course, is reversed; they exhort the gullible *not* to buy. Buy not Judaism—it is un-Christian, it is conspiratorial, it is aggressive, it is out to overpower you, and so on.

These hate vendors, cunning in their business, invariably attach the words "Christian," "Cross," "Crusade," or some denominational adjective to the name of their organization. Knowing the value of the traditional attitude of disdain toward Jews embodied in these terms, they start off with the asset of being "Christian gentlemen."

Most of the American and British professional anti-Semitic agitators were ne'er-do-wells with little imagination who hit upon familiar church anti-Semitism as a ready product, adding other borrowed accusations as they went along.

They could never command a notable following since they were uninspired and unconvinced, hence uninspiring and unconvincing. They attracted odd little groups of walking inferiority complexes who yearned for snappy belts and boots. Occasionally they would persuade some elderly man of wealth to contribute to their support. In the long run, their campaigns dwindle to smearing walls with swastikas, overturning Jewish tombstones, and modeling their operetta uniforms like degenerate exhibitionists.

DOMINICANS

were the most vicious of the Catholic orders. Their privileged position in the Inquisition was only a small part of their war against the Jews.

Consciously or by conditioned reflex, they never failed to include the Jews in their sermons against infidels and heretics.

In 1422, Dominicans led a fierce campaign against the Hussite heresy in Bohemia. They spiced their sermons with deadly accusations against the Jews: drinking blood from Christian corpses, driving nails through consecrated wafers representing the host, and poisoning wine and water. The masses of Christians, having no other tutors but the clergy, were kept in a furious heat against the Christ killers.

The Dominican preachers openly invoked their Christian assemblies to violence and the destruction of Jewish property. Their slogan, deep into the eighteenth century, was: "Why seek for the enemies of Christ if His killers are right among us?"

In similar manner, the Nazi troops en route to fight their traditional enemies in France, Poland and Russia paused to massacre Jews as the absolute enemy of a Christian Germany.

DOMUS CONVERSORUM

A conversion mill established 1232 in London by Henry III. The campaign was of little consequence since in 1290 all Jews were expelled from England.

DREYFUS CASE

The notorious framing of the Jewish Captain Alfred Dreyfus was possible only because of the deep anti-Semitic sentiment of the French clergy (Edouard Drumont, etc.). The Catholic press, and indeed almost all Catholic opinion, was committed to support of the frame-up. Its exposure caused irreparable damage to the political influence of the clergy in France.

DRUMONT, EDOUARD

French anti-Semite who in his *La France Juive* (1886) attributed all ills of Christian France to the Jews. Even rising anticlericalism was "created by Jewish power." His writings, widely distributed by a gullible clergy, helped to create the background for the Dreyfus frame-up.

DU MONTFORT, FATHER (1673-1716)

Influential Catholic priest in Brittany, who wrote and composed a great number of popular religious songs shot through with anti-Semitic offense: "Jewish barbarians broke his limbs, they cut his flesh, they bared his nerves, they . . ."

These pious songs are still being chanted in the French countryside.

DUNS SCOTUS, JOHN (1266-1308)

English Franciscan monk and renowned theologian, who "proved with convincing logic" that not only was it a privilege but a duty of the Catholic Church to take away the children of reluctant Jewish parents and forcibly baptize them. Also, the parents should be compelled by all means to convert. Any such efforts would be true piety—so philosophized "the Doctor Subtilis."

E

ECK, JOHANN VON (1486-1543)

German Catholic theologian and one of the chief opponents of Lutheranism; vehemently attacked all secular authorities that tolerated Jews in their territories.

While Von Eck disagreed with Luther on all major ecclesiastical issues, in matters Judaica they concurred.

An epigone, the Jesuit Adam Contzen (1570-1635) of Mainz, called the Jews "poisonous animals" who should be hounded into oblivion. Contzen was Professor of Moral (*sic!*) Theology at the university.

ECUMENICAL CLIMATE

Pope Paul VI, cunctator of ecumenism, directed the proper Vatican secretariat to cooperate with Protestant translators of the New Testament, and we shall have another English version of the Greek text.

From the efforts of Wycliffe (whose corpse was desecrated by the clergy) and Tyndale (who was burned by the Church) to the Catholic Douai Bible and the King James Version, the differences in the Christian canon and legend are minimal.

The last few decades have burgeoned with philological attempts to interpret the New Testament, by Catholics and Protestants alike. Like their predecessors, the current translators use either the Greek editions or the Vulgata, a Latin text prepared from the Greek.

But neither Jesus, His Apostles nor His followers spoke Greek or Latin—they spoke Hebrew. When speaking of peace, the great ecumenic theme, Jesus said not *"Eirene,"* nor did He say *"Pax."* He said *"Shalom."*

And while the Catholics, true to the doctrine of the "perpetual virginity of Mary," contrary to the Protestant theologians, refer to Christ's brothers as "brethren," Christ's kin were, and because of ecumenic superficiality, still are subject to derision and hate in the very Gospels that bespeak His love.

No matter in what linguistic or doctrinal detail Catholics and Protestants differ, they all agree to retain in the coming Gospel translation the naming of *"The* Jews" as sons of the Devil, bloodthirsty tormenters and killers of Christ, idolators of a God-accursed religion!

This last curse against the Jews was repeated only months after the end of Vatican II by none other than Bishop Luigi Carli, the appointee of Paul VI to head the Ecumenical Curia dealing with the Jews and Judaism.

As long as the Christian theologians are unwilling to excise these ugly references to the people of Jesus from their canon, it will remain a book of death to the Jews, even if the new translators succeed in recruiting a few "Uncle Tom" Jews to participate in their "ecumenic committee."

There can be no real ecumenism with "sons of the Devil," and so we are described in the New Testament.

Someday, in the distant future, we hope there will arise a true concept of brotherhood even among the Christians and they will cease teaching their young that the Children of Israel are diabolical God killers.

Someday the Christians will learn that if God considered the Jews a devil's brood, He would not have sent His only Son to be born among them, from the womb of a Jewish mother.

Such a canon is not of God; the mark on the forehead of the Jewish nation as it appears in the Gospels was placed there not by Him but by Satan.

EISENMENGER, JOHANN ANDREAS (1654-1704)

Lutheran and anti-Semitic agitator. His book, *Entdecktes Judentum,* has served as an arsenal of anti-Semitic calumny since 1700.

ELVIRA, COUNCIL OF

Banned (306 A.D.) all community contact between Spanish Christians and the evil Hebrews; prohibited marriage of Christians and Jews (cf. racial purity laws of Nazism).

EMANCIPATION

of the Jewish people in Christian countries received its great impetus with the American and French revolutions. America led by a hundred years all other nations. Here is a partial chronology of freedom:

1636, Rhode Island granted religious liberty.
1669, "Jews, heathens and dissenters," granted liberty of conscience in the Carolinas.
1777, Constitution of New York State placed Jews on a status of complete equality with other residents.
1781, Joseph of Austria abolishes poll tax and issues "Toleranz patent."
1786, Religious liberty granted Jews in Hungary.
1788, Poll tax abolished in Prussia.
1790, French National Assembly grants citizenship to Bordeaux Sephardim.
1791, French National Assembly grants equality to the Jews.
1796, Batavian National Assembly grants equality to Netherlands Jews.
1806, Napoleon's Assembly of Jewish notables held.
1807, Session of Napoleon's Sanhedrin.
1808, Jews of Westphalia and of Baden emancipated.
1811, Jews of Hamburg emancipated.
1812, Jews of Mecklenburg-Prussia emancipated.
1830, Abolition of More Judaico (Jewish oath) in France.
1831, Emancipation of Jews of Jamaica.
1833, Emancipation of Jews of Hesse.
1846, "Toleration Tax," abolished in Hungary.

1848, Emancipation of Jews of German States.
1849, Jews of Denmark emancipated.
1858, Jewish disabilities removed in England.
1859, Equality granted in Italy.
1860, Austrian Jews emancipated.
1861. Jewish oath abolished and Jews emancipated in Württemberg.
1865, Disabilities removed in Sweden.
1865, Complete equality granted in Belgium.
1866, Emancipation of Jews in Switzerland.
1867, Emancipation of the Jews in Hungary.
1869, Jews granted political equality in Prussia.
1872, Bavarian Jews emancipated.
1904, More Judaica abolished in Rumania.
1905-6, Jews granted political rights in Russian Empire.
1908, Jews granted political rights in Turkish Empire.
1919, All citizens equalized in U.S.S.R.
1919, Jews granted equality in Rumania, Poland, Latvia, Lithuania, Czechoslovakia, Yugoslavia.
1932. Equality of all citizens granted in Spain.

ENDLOESUNG

"The final solution" of the "Jewish problem," so well known through the Nuremberg and Tel-Aviv trials, never fully materialized for the Hitler-Himmler-Eichmann group, as it did not fully materialize for King Ferdinand and Queen Isabella or the Catholic royalty of Portugal, France and England.

All expelled some Jews and murdered others who stood by Judaism.

Somehow the Jews remained, as Saint Augustinus said, *"necessarii credentibus gentibus,"* historical witness to Christian salvation.

Germany came closest to *Endlösung* under Catholicism after the Black Death era which followed the Crusade massacres, the Rindfleisch butchery, the well-poisoning killings and the ritual murder bloodbath. By 1500 Catholic Germany was *judenfrei*, as were France and of course England.

The Jews perished by tens of thousands, hundreds of thousands, men, women and children, under the ax and the sword and the torch, drowned, quartered, burned, garroted, knifed and stuck like pigs.

Israel was at the mercy of the Catholic Church and there was no mercy—this was a Christian world and, as Hitler later explained, there was no room for the *"Pariah-volk."*

It was the people of Jesus, His mother's people, Joseph's kin, whom the Catholics murdered. From the Ebro to the Elbe, from the Tiber to the Seine and Thames, all the rivers of Europe received the blood of Israel, of Christ's Israel, His Apostles' Israel—the blood of the direct descendants of all those who erected in the Judean hills the great edifice of Christendom.

Israel had to die because the Romans would not tolerate a king of the Jews. What irony and what tragedy!

And it was the Teutons, Iberians, Gauls and sundry Visigoths who drew the blood of Christ's very kin! The barbarians in bearskins who were living a savage life when the Psalms were written by David, the kingly bard, whose ancestry the evangelists claimed for Jesus—it was these barbarians who won the blessing of the Church as they ripped the holy scrolls of Judea and punished with fire and crimson swords the People of God, the People of the Book, the People of Christ.

The Catholic Church failed to obliterate the perennial seed of the Holy Land, and the Nazi Teutons failed, but Israel was left a much reduced nation.

We cannot deny that the Church and the Nazi Germans have done us grievous and permanent damage. Our children have fallen away in front of our eyes, and our women been tortured to death, even more by the Church than by the modern savages.

It may be thousands of miles away where this happened,

65

and a thousand years ago. But my kin was thus brutalized by the pretenders to Christ, and there is no example in all history, primitive or civilized, of men doing to men for centuries what Christians have done to Jews.

And there is no end in sight since the Church refuses to change a word of its precious catechisms and codes and dogmas and scripture. To the church the word is sacrosanct, but the life of a Jew is just a Jew's life.

ENGLISH LITERATURE

The Canterbury Tales (1386) by Chaucer is one of many classical literary pieces with a Christian anti-Semitic motif—in this case the depicting of a Jew as a vampire. With typical Christian malevolence of the time, the Jew is styled a member of that "God accursed" race. Such literary pieces, imbued with direct or indirect Jew hatred, have done much to keep anti-Semitism alive by a kind of subliminal effect.

Marlowe joined the same sad literary clique with his play, *The Jew of Malta* (1592). Marlowe's villain is a monstrous Jew who revels in the killing of Christians, by well poisoning or plain murder.

Shakespeare followed the easy road to public appeal in his *Merchant of Venice* (1597) by switching the characters of a Venetian tale. In the Venetian tale the flesh-greedy merchant is a Christian who makes a wager with a Jew against a pound of the Jew's flesh. Shakespeare simply reversed the roles and made the Jew an ogre.

English anti-Semitism was kept alive by a surly clergy. Chaucer, Marlowe and Shakespeare could never have come across a single Jew, since the Jews had been expelled from England in 1290. They were not permitted entry until 1659, by Oliver Cromwell, who got his edict through Parliament in spite of a venomously Jew-hating clergy. The English had forsaken Catholicism, but not its Jew hatred.

Essayists like Charles Lamb (1823) berated the Jews

viciously for "killing Christ." Even children's literature has been poisoned by the Gospel image of the Jew as a money-changer and Judas. In Grimm's German *Fairy Tales* a story, "The Jew in the Bush," stars a cheat, thief and scoundrel, a Jew who winds up on the gallows.

Not even the "Mother Goose" verses escaped the Sunday school venom:

"Jack sold his egg to a rogue of a Jew,
Who cheated him out of half his due."

It took the advent of the Giant Killer Hitler to remove these references from the American editions. Other Christian nations still perpetuate them, as British dictionaries still define "Jew" in the old Church manner: a cheat, a disreputable trader.

EPHRAEM, SAINT (306-373)

Highly regarded in the Eastern Church, refers in his hymns to the synagogues as whorehouses.

EPHRAIM OF JERUSALEM

This benign patriarch, passing through Bucharest (1764-66) ordered Prince Alexander Glinka to demolish the synagogue. It was done.

EPIPHANIUS, SAINT (310-403)

In his histories of heresies mentioned dishonesty and indolence as typical Jewish characteristics.

ERFURT

In this German town on June 26, 1221, a band of pilgrims from Friesland bound for the Holy Land stormed the Jewish quarter and killed twenty-six Hebrews. For hundreds of years this pious victory was commemorated. But it was made insignificant by the murder of three thousand Jews in August, 1348, as poisoners of wells. The accusations were spread by Dominican monks of the city.

ERWIG (680-687)

This Spanish King was a most pious ruler who made twenty-eight anti-Jewish regulations into law. The Twelfth Council of Toledo (681) approved all of them. In 694 the Seventeenth Council of Toledo, together with this noble King, reduced all Jews to servitude, prohibiting their religious rites, and ordained that all Jewish children above seven be taken from their parents and converted to the Cross.

ESTELLA

Through this and other Spanish towns bordering France, the Franciscan friar, Peter Olligen, wandered in 1328, preaching in churches against the God killers. Thousands of Jews were martyred.

ETHIOPIA

In the second half of the nineteenth century European missionaries appeared in Addis Ababa and began an intensive campaign against the native Jews (Falashas) who had been living there for more than a thousand years. They failed to break the spirit of the Falashas; however, some of the Ethiopian Jews attempted to flee to Palestine (1868).

EUGENIUS III

Pope (1145-1153); offered mercenary Crusaders, as an enlistment inducement, absolution from any debt owed to Jews.

EUSEBIUS

Bishop of Caesarea who flourished around 300, maintained that the Jews in every community crucified a Christian at their Purim festival as a rejection of Jesus. This kindly saint also asserted that during the Roman-Persian war the Jews purchased ninety thousand Christian prisoners merely for the pleasure of killing them. His *Ecclesiastic History* is standard in Catholic libraries.

EVIAN

Site of conference called in 1938 to discuss the problem of Jewish escape from Nazi Germany, attended by representatives from thirty-two countries. No help was given the Jews.

The German Protestant and Catholic Church leaders were rapidly integrating their activities with the newly formed Nazi organizations. To the Jews of Germany all doors of escape were shut, as were all doors of entry in the rest of the world.

EVORA

In this Portuguese city in 1497 the Catholic authorities under King Manuel issued the edict that all Jewish children under fourteen years be taken from their parents and distributed by parish priests among Christian parents.

In April 1506, the only synagogue in town was destroyed. A generation later the Catholic Inquisition of Portugal began its murderous work here.

EXCHEQUER JEWS

A term coined by King Frederick Barbarossa, who placed the Jews of the Rhineland in fortresses to protect them against the Crusaders of the Catholic Church, claiming that the Hebrews belonged to his "private exchequer."

Upon occasion, other rulers of Europe also tried to protect their industrious and skilled Jewish subjects from the fury of the Church.

For example, Philip Augustus of France (1181-1223) fought tooth and nail with his barons for the possession of the Jews—artisans, traders, and manufacturers alike—since, like his royal fellows, he drew great profits from the talent of the Jews.

Unfortunately, monks and priests from the bishops on down, enflamed by their own hateful liturgy and litany, constantly pushed for the death or conversion of Jews. To placate the powerful church, or whenever it suited them, the rulers would drop the Jews. The Church was ever ready to take over and lead the mob against the marked Jews, trapped in their ghettos.

EXISTENTIALISM, CHRISTIAN

has in Martin Heidegger its most influential representative. Catholic and Protestant seminaries alike have adopted the body of thought of this philosopher, making it predominant in their classrooms and manifestos. Here is what the Christian existentialist has to say:

"The Führer himself, and only he, is the current and future reality of Germany, and his word is your law.

"There exists only one single German way of life, a way whose enrichment is being shaped in the National Socialist Revolution. *Heil Hitler*."

F

FAGIN

The tendency of a popular writer to ingratiate himself with a wide public by pandering to their prejudices is readily discernible in this figure of a wicked "fence" created by Charles Dickens in his novel, *Oliver Twist*. The Christian churches had popularized the image of Judas. The very

Gospels, in their Romanized editions, take advantage of the word play that marks the traitor Judas as a Jew, although Jesus and the Apostles also were Jews. In most catechisms the Jewishness of Gospel heroes is ignored and that of Judas stressed.

Prejudice, originally nurtured in the world of the Christian religion, does not end there. Its fictional image becomes imbedded in a secular canon consisting of literary classics and thence finds its way into common speech. Consider the definition of Fagin to be found, a century and more after the publication of *Oliver Twist,* in a current American dictionary: "adult who instructs others in crime, especially one who teaches children to steal."

FAULHABER, CARDINAL MICHAEL VON (1869-1952)

in his notorious Advent sermon of 1933, defended the Old Testament, but attacked the Jews of his day and disavowed any impression that he was pleading their case against the threats of Hitlerism.

A leading article in *Klerusblatt,* organ of the Bavarian Priests Association, followed the "Christian" sermon of Faulhaber by admonishing Catholic teachers to point out to their pupils that the Old Testament, sacred to Christians, was in direct conflict with "current" "Jewish" mentality.

FERRER, SAINT VINCENT

Dominican itinerant preacher (1350-1419) who traveled with a retinue of three hundred Flagellants. In his zeal for the conversion of Jews he was responsible for their incarceration and severe punishment. He whipped up the populace to intense hatred and suspicion of the Jews, which culminated in the promulgation of the Castilian Edict (January 12, 1412), containing twenty-four articles *contra Judaeos,* among them the creation of ghettos in all Spanish towns.

FERRIOL, SAINT

In 561 this Bishop of Uzes, France, gave the Jews a choice: baptism or exile.

FICHTE, JOHANN GOTTLIEB (1762-1814)

German nationalist philosopher and Protestant theologian with strong anti-Semitic tendencies.

"FINAL SOLUTION"

See *Endlösung*

FLAGELLANTS

in fourteenth-century France and Germany were driven by two "religious" motivations: self-abuse and Jew-abuse.

FLEMISH CHURCH SHOWS

in the Middle Ages exhibited a Jew astride a billy goat, the symbol of devilish lechery. Such portrayals have been preserved in church sculpture and pictures.

FOETOR JUDAICUS

or Jewish Satanic stench, widely popularized by priests and monks; can only be washed away by baptism (Convention of Clermont, 576). German Nazis made similar charges of *foetor judaicus*.

FOURIER, CHARLES (1772-1837)

Raised in a Catholic parochial school, the son of one of the very wealthy merchants of France, he managed to dissipate his fortune and spent his life attacking everything mercantile.

His Church-injected Jew hatred made him single out the Hebrew people as devoid of all patriotism and culture. The Jews were traitors because of Judas; they were usurers because of the papal bulls; they were immoral and should be isolated from all Christians (the ghetto).

While Fourier in his mature years lost all interest in Christian theology, the Church anti-Semitism of his childhood continued to pervade his outlook.

FRANCE

First in 1306 and again in 1394 Jews were expelled from France. As in England, the clergy never flagged in its relentless anti-Semitic pressure upon king and counselors.

On May, 1615, the Parliament of Paris, under severe pressure by the Bishop, reinstated the 1394 edict of expulsion of all Jews under pain of death.

FRANKFORT PURIM

Lutheran pogrom, on Purim in 1612, of the Jewish ghetto, led by the fanatical rabble-rouser Fettmilch. He took Luther's anti-Semitic orders literally.

FREDERICK AUGUSTUS I

Saxon King of Poland between 1697 and 1733, permitted the Catholic clergy to enforce the Council of Basel decree that compelled Jews to listen in their synagogues to "conversion sermons." In some instances the Church had to call out the army to enforce attendance (Lvov, 1721). The Catholic Church, with the help of a greedy nobility, instituted most burdensome ordinances and restrictions upon the Jews. In 1720 the Catholic Synod of Lovich prohibited the Jews from building new synagogues or repairing old ones.

Under Frederick Augustus II the Catholic Church went one step further by reissuing at Plozk (1733) the edict:

"The Jews should be only tolerated as a reminder of the suffering of Christ and in their position as serfs serve as an example of God's punishment of infidels."

With this horrid upsurge of Catholic anti-Semitism—which, incidentally, never left Poland—accusations against Jews as child murderers, well poisoners, blood drinkers, and host desecraters became a daily occurrence. Hebrew prayer books were confiscated and burned in Kamenetz-Podolsk by the Catholic clergy under the leadership of Archbishop Dembovsky.

FREDERICK THE GREAT (1740-1786)

The philosopher-king of Prussia proved clearly that a man can be a liberal on many levels and still be an anti-Semite.

His rigid Protestant Church school training was not lost on this monarch. He forbade immigration of Jews and restricted Jewish families to one child. He found various pretexts under which to extract protection money from the Jews, such as toll taxes on cattle, etc.

It was only the Napoleonic era that brought the Jews of Germany and Austria a respite from degradation.

FREEMASONRY

In the official *Dictionnaire apologétique de la foi catholique,* now in print, this is written about the Jews under the above heading:

"In the mind of Satan, the synagogue has an immense place. The Devil relies on the Jews to govern Freemasonry. The Jewish brain directs the action against the Church, the Pope, Christ. Crucify Him! Crucify Him!"

The editor of the *Dictionnaire* is Père d'Alès, S.J., professor at the Catholic Institute of Paris.

Julius Streicher in his *Stürmer* used almost identical phraseology.

FRENCH CATHOLICISM

Chaplains of the armed forces of Vichy France were prohibited by the Catholic Church from serving in the Partisan forces of the Free French during World War II. Most Catholic bishops remained loyal to the Nazi-supported Pétain "government" and denounced all its opponents as "rebels." The record of Catholic clerical collaboration with Hitlerism was assembled in *The French Catholics Under the Occupation*, a book by the liberal Catholic journalist, Jacques Duquesne.

During the years of the Nazi Occupation, the majority of the French clergy interpreted France's military defeat as "a just punishment" for the country's abandonment to "Jewish Freemasonry." Hitler appears as the punishing arm of the Lord, much like the pagan Emperor Titus of Rome, whose destruction of Jerusalem was interpreted as Divine vengeance for the crucifixion. Especially during Holy Week, the Catholic clergy in France as well as Germany stressed, not the bestiality of Nazism, but rather "the cruelty of the Jews toward the Savior."

FRENCH POLL

of 1966 on anti-Semitism, conducted by the French Institute of Public Opinion, showed that most of French prejudice toward the Jews sprang from early Church teaching and was strongest in communities where no Jews existed at all.

Half of the Frenchmen polled would oppose a Jewish President; one-third would never vote for a Jewish representative. Almost half of the Frenchmen polled consider the participation of Jews in the country's industrial and commercial life as an evil; 20 percent would not consult a Jewish doctor in fear of being poisoned, while more than 33 percent would never work for a Jew.

Needless to say, these prejudices can be traced back to

the thousand-year-old religious instruction in anti-Semitism preached by the Catholic Church and its parochial schools.

FRENCH REVOLUTION

Catholic clergy, through provincial representatives, made strenuous efforts to stop the granting of civil rights to the Jews by the National Assembly.

FRIES, JAKOB FRIEDRICH (1773-1843)

Sentimental German philosopher and theologian who suggested that all new-born Jewish infants be thrown into rivers, as a simple solution to the "Jewish problem."

FUEHRER JESUS

"The Führer of every Christian is Jesus Christ, the Führer of every German is Adolf Hitler."—Society of National Socialist Priests and Ministers, signed: Rev. Paul Fiebig, 1940.

G

GAYRAUD, HIPPOLYTE

Dominican monk, professor of theology, who promoted "Christian anti-Semitism"—as if there were any other. Father Gayraud declared: "A convinced Christian is by nature a practicing anti-Semite." At the first Congress of the Christian Democrats in Lyon (1896), he clamored that the Catholic Church has always been anti-Semitic "on a high moral [!] plane."

GELBE FLECK (Yellow Badge)

The yellow band issued by the Hitler Germans, with or without the Star of David, has its origin in an edict of the

Catholic Church. It was promulgated during the Fourth Lateran Council convoked by Pope Innocent III in 1215. The Jews were ordered to wear a distinctive dress. A comparable badge or dress of shame was also prescribed for prostitutes and lepers. Medieval illustrations frequently show the Devil with the Jew badge.

These badges of shame imposed upon Jews by the Vatican took many forms in different lands: hats, armbands, circlets. They made Jewish men, women and children easy marks for attack, under the Nazis as under the Church authorities.

GELEITGELD

"Protection money" which Jews had to pay to the local abbot or noble in Germany. This was paid in addition to the poll tax.

These fees were extracted from the Jews until the end of the eighteenth century, when the French Revolutionary armies arrived and liberated them from this oppression.

GENOCIDE

was preached a thousand years before the Germans ran amuck in their Jew hatred. The Church-inspired Crusaders put to death or caused the suicide of more than one-third of the Hebrew population in Central Europe in the eleventh century. When Emperor Henry IV issued an edict permitting the forcibly converted to return to the faith of their fathers, Pope Clement III forbade, under dire threats, such disregard of holy baptism.

GENUFLECTING

in a manner to ridicule Jesus has been attributed by Catholic liturgy to the Jews. In fact, this was done by the Roman soldiers, not the Jews. (See Matthew 27:27-29.)

GERMAN CATHOLICISM

In a prearranged conference on April 26, 1933, between German Chancellor Adolf Hitler and Catholic Bishop Wilhelm Berning, Hitler stressed the fundamental agreement between National Socialism and Catholicism on the "Jewish question."

At the conference Hitler affirmed that "the Catholic Church had always regarded Jews as evildoers [*Schädlinge*] and had banished them into ghettos. He [Hitler] is only doing what the Church had been doing for fifteen hundred years."

This and a number of other conferences led to the infamous Concordat of Collaboration between Berlin and Rome, a crowning achievement for the Papal Nuncio, Msgr. Pacelli, later Pope Pius XII. The signing of the Concordat gave an imprimatur to Hitler's terror regime.

At a time when the whole civilized world stood aghast at the rising Brown Dragon, the Vatican put its seal of approval on this band of bloodthirsty political adventurers who promised in all their declarations, including *Mein Kampf,* to annihilate every Jewish man, woman and child.

Was not Hitler confirmed, then, in his statement that he was only doing on a systematic scale what the Catholic Church had been doing all along?

Some incidents in the enforcement of Brown Catholicism:

Except in Bishop Konrad von Preysing's See of Berlin, all—but all—Catholic diocesan publications carried Herr Goebbels' propaganda articles, including those of vilest anti-Semitic tone.

The bells of all Catholic churches in Hitler's Germany rang jubilantly at the "annexation" of Austria. In Austria itself Theodor Cardinal Innitzer appealed to the populace to "approve" the union. The Cardinal signed this appeal: "Heil Hitler."

On April 20, 1939, on the occasion of Hitler's fiftieth birthday, all Catholic churches—but all, without exception

78

—raised the Nazi hooked cross in celebration. This was a voluntary gesture of solidarity accompanied by telegrams of felicitation to "the protector of the Reich" from all but two of the bishops.

Long before, in 1934, Archbishop Gröder ordered that the swastika be raised next to the Church flag on all patriotic occasions.

In October, 1939, Adolf Cardinal Bertram asked all dioceses to ring their church bells at the expected fall of Warsaw. Reverend Hans Kerrl, Minister for Religious Affairs, had given similar instructions to the Protestant clergy.

God was on the side of Hitler; the Christian church leaders placed Him there. Never mind the half-million Jews of Warsaw, the kin of Jesus.

Then, as now, the kin of Jesus were pariahs forever beyond pity, be they women or children or invalids, to be hated, accursed. "They pushed for the death of Christ," as the Vatican Council has so distinctly declared. "They," *the* Jews, pushed for the death of Christ; for Hitler "they," *the* Jews, were the root of all evil.

Hitlerism and Catholicism, two movements that joined so harmoniously in one purpose, both condemned the Jews as such.

Jesus said, "Let the children come unto me," and the Christian churches let a million Jewish children come unto the Devil himself, who choked them to death with his noxious fumes and then burned their pain-twisted bodies like foul meat.

Meanwhile the Christian clerics hailed the antichrist with hymns, blessings and bells from one end of Europe to the other.

The Pope had made a concordat with the Devil, and both kept their bargain.

Hitler is dead, but Catholicism still cries out for the blood of Israel amid its pretentious Ecumenism: The Jews pushed for the death of Christ.

Hitler is dead, but Christian anti-Semitism is very much

alive, and the teachings that nurtured Nazism are still being repeated in Christian churches, and in religious schools. They preach the same old Gospel that the Jews are the sons of the Devil, that the Jews have bloody hands, that the Jews wanted to break the dying Jesus' bones, that the Jews are betrayers of God, that the Jews are accursed by the Lord and that they desecrate the temples.

Nothing has changed to stop another Hitler from rising. The Christians need a Devil for their liturgy, and the Jew suits them well.

GERMAN PROTESTANTISM

Its founder was the rebellious monk, Martin Luther (1483-1546), who gave Hitler his basic program: Get rid of the Jews and take their possessions. In Luther's words: "Take all their coins and jewels, silver and gold . . . [let] their synagogues and schools be set afire, their houses be broken up—[let] them be put under a roof or stable like gypsies."

It is noteworthy that Hitler followed these directions implicitly, even including the gypsies in his master plan.

The Protestant clergy in Germany welcomed and supported National Socialism. After Hitler's election a new Protestant Reich Church was formed. The German Protestants made Hitler's confidant, Chaplain Ludwig Mueller, the new head of their church. In July, 1935, Hitler appointed Hans Kerrl to be Minister for Church Affairs. With very few exceptions the Protestant pastors fell in line. Anti-Semitism, a traditional Lutheran tenet enlarged only in detail by Hitler, won their overwhelming support.

In the ten long years of dominant National Socialism, which of the ten thousand German churches, chapels, Sunday schools, and meeting houses, heard an appeal from the Protestant clergy to stop the torture and suffocation of Jewish children, women and unarmed men?

It is wrong, it is false history, to lay the blame for criminal indifference to the slaughter of Jews only upon

Catholics and their stony Pope. The Protestant church of Germany was thoroughly Lutheran in its anti-Semitism. When the Nazis placed the Jews in ghetto stables and camps, they only followed Luther's precept; when they burned Jewish synagogues, homes and schools, they only carried out Luther's will; when the Germans robbed the Jews of their possessions and heritage, they only did Luther's bidding; when the Germans reduced Jews to concentration camp slavery, they merely followed the teaching of Luther: Make the Hebrews slaves of the serfs!

There was no anti-Semitic crime prescribed by Luther that the Germans failed to carry out, and there was no crime perpetrated by the Nazis that Luther had not ordered in his book, *Die Juden und ihre Lügen.*

GERMAN THEOLOGIANS

Protestant as well as Catholic, they were almost to a man vociferously anti-Semitic: Schleiermacher, Hegel, Herder and Harnack are just a few of those who held the libel of the Jews as God killer to be Gospel truth.

GHETTO

For a Jew to leave the ghetto was punishable by death under Hans Frank, Nazi Governor of Poland. This, of course, was only a repetition of a similar papal ruling of 1215. How time crawls!

GLYATOVSKY, JANNIKI (d. 1668)

Russian Orthodox cleric who wrote a widely publicized pamphlet, *Messia Pravdivi,* against Judaism.

GOBINEAU, ARTHUR (1816-1882)

Early French racialist and anti-Semite, who took his main concept from the Catholic blood-purists of fifteenth-century Spain (Alfonso de Spina). Gobineau's *Essay on the Inequality of Human Races* greatly stimulated Alfred Rosenberg.

GOD IS DEAD

The basic and most fundamental dogma of all Christianity.

God died and left His Son's Testament in a Greek translation (no Hebrew text has ever been found, yet neither Jesus nor the Apostles wrote or spoke anything but Hebrew), to be followed implicitly.

If the New Testament states that the Jews are the Sons of the Devil and are bloodthirsty, treacherous, the killers of God and thus forever accursed, this is Gospel truth, the Word of God.

The dogma of the Jews' deviltry is incontestable since God Himself no longer makes changes; indeed, He is dead and left the Gospels as His heritage to the Christian churches.

No group or nation or alliance of nations in all known history has ever perpetrated on a hapless minority such sadistic atrocities over so long a time as the Christians have on the Jews.

Not one denomination or another, but *all* did, and especially those of the Catholic faith: They have choked to death little children in the presence of their parents to make them denounce their fathers and mothers as well poisoners, as blood drinkers, as plague carriers. They have shriveled the naked breasts of women with hot irons to make them betray their husbands as breakers of holy wafers. They have stretched the bodies of fathers on the rack to make them denounce their own flesh and blood as false converts.

What the Germans did to six million Jews in the Second World War is only a continuation of long-established Christian bestiality toward the Jewish people, practiced by European Christians and especially the Catholic Church every decade of every century for the last two thousand years.

If the Christians believed in God, they could never have perpetrated or tolerated the monstrous deeds they did to the Jews. But they think God dead. Neither do they believe in the resurrection. They believe only in the Greek book put together in the fourth century, from some fragmentary scrolls, by a church made dominant in the Roman Empire by the pagan king, Constantine, who in all his days never accepted their faith for himself.

If they believed in the resurrection, how could they face the returned Jesus after all the unspeakable cruelties they inflicted on his people? Jesus had brothers and sisters, cousins and uncles, distant kin and friends who remained Jews in the land of Israel. What became of their descendants? They left for many lands as did their Apostolic brethren—to Iberia, to Gaul, to Germany, to the north and the west. What did the Christians do to them? The Christians tormented them during the Crusades, the Inquisition, and a thousand times in a thousand towns and villages.

How could the Christians face Jesus after what they did to his kin and the kin of the Holy Mother Mary and the kin of Joseph?

But the Christians did what they did because they believed neither in God nor in His Son. They thought Him dead, and the Holy Spirit a mere dream.

What they have left is a Greek book, and the best part of it, in which they all take delight no matter how they may disagree on details of liturgy, is: The Jews be damned! The choice part about the Jew as Devil, no one can take that out of their Greek book. That is Gospel truth, that is divine inspiration, that is God's word!

You can't question a dogma, they say, and the hate passages in the New Testament are God's word. They have to stay there, these poisonous little accusations, and innuendoes: Jews are Sons of the Devil, Jews are bloody killers of Christ, Jews are betrayers of God, Jews are condemned forever, Jews are spitters on God, torturers of

God, breakers of God's dying bones! Even the youngest infant born yesterday in a Jewish home is accursed forever. *Pereat Judea!*

GOD'S SPY

On February 15, 1898, the *Civiltà Cattolica* had written that "the Jew was created by God to serve as a spy wherever treason is brewing. First economic, anti-Semitism will become what it must be, political and national."

GOOD FRIDAY

is the unholiest day of the Christian calendar: it serves not to commemorate the Hebraic message of Love as expressed by the gentle Jew of Nazareth, but rather the Roman Church philosophy of vindictive and hateful revenge on the descendants of an ancient nation where an alleged jury of a few elders "ordered" a man—and Jesus was a man then—to be tried by the local Roman security chief on the charge of impersonating Caesar.

Good Friday is the day when Christians in sermons, lectures and "passion plays," berate and befoul everything Jewish. With devious art and cunning, the agonies of crucifixion are again described, depicted and relived—although the Christians themselves in the centuries of their history have tortured to death not one Hebrew, but ten million of them, including at least a million infants and children who were of the same flesh and blood as the noble Jesus ben Joseph.

It is not the Roman-style execution which Jesus suffered, together with thousands of other Jews, at the hands of the conquerors of Israel that is worthy of remembrance after all these centuries, but rather the Hebraic precept of Love of Man, even Man the Stranger and Man the Enemy.

Is it not time to cease the sanctimonious dramatizing of one man's pain, to drop the hypocritical self-righteousness and smug "empathy" with the Son of God, whose Hebrew mother and father-in-flesh are still subject to vile hate and vituperation in their surviving kinfolk?

It seems these militant Christians want forever to strut the broad parade-ground of hate rather than seek the narrow path of love.

GOUGENOT DES MOUSSEUX, HENRI

French anti-Semite of the late nineteenth century, author of *Le Juif, le judaisme et la judaisation des peuples chrétiens,* published on the eve of the Vatican Council (1870). Gougenot was a most influential Catholic lay leader, a daily (!) communicant, whose malevolent book was prefaced by Father Voisin, director of the Catholic Foreign Mission in Paris. Pope Pius IX gave author and book his blessing.

Gougenot blamed the defeat of Catholic Austria by the Protestant Prussians on the Jews, an example Hitler followed by blaming the Jews for Germany's defeat in World War I.

GREGORY I (540-604)

This anti-Semitic Pope has been referred to by many as "the Great." He called Judaism a superstitious, perfidious and depraved belief. He praised the Visigothic King Reccared for his severity in anti-Semitic regulations. He proposed many cruel edicts against the Jews, depriving them of their civil rights.

GREGORY XIII (1502-1585)

Among the bulls of this Pope: compelled the Jews of Rome to maintain a house of conversion (1578); prohibited Jewish physicians from attending Christian patients (1581); appropriated from the Jews all their canon literature (1581); ordered Jews to listen to abusive anti-Semitic conversion sermons every Saturday in their own synagogues (1584).

GREGORY OF NYSSA, SAINT (331-396)

called the Jews assassins of the prophets, companions of the Devil, a race of vipers, a sanhedrin of demons, enemies of all that is beautiful, and more—not all of it printable.

He and Saint John Chrysostom, who in loving brotherliness styled the Jews "hogs and goats in their lewd grossness," are the most outstanding of the Byzantine Church anti-Semites, who were largely responsible for the fear and disdain in which the Jews were held in the Russian Empire.

GROEBER, ARCHBISHOP KONRAD

of the German Rhine provinces, in his pastoral letter of March, 1941, to the clergy in his diocese, attacked the Jews along simple Nazi propaganda lines, winding up with a reference to Christ killers and adding that whatever happens to the Jews is only the fulfillment of God's vengeance —making Hitler the right arm of the Lord.

GRODNO

In this Polish (now Russian) town Jesuits arrived in 1616, with wild anti-Semitic accusations of host desecration and blood orgies. The last ritual-murder scare in this town, inspired as always by the low clergy, occurred in 1820.

GUI, BERNARD (d. 1331)

Author of one of the many "manuals of inquisition" which gave hints on how to spot a Jew or a "backsliding" convert and how to extend and intensify the suffering of the interrogated by flame, garrote, rack, whip and needle.

A number of priests were always present, crucifix in hand, to take down the "confessions" of the agonized Jews. Children were customarily martyred in front of their fettered parents.

Cardinal Francisco Jiménez de Cisneros and Cardinal Juan de Torquemada, who burned nine thousand Jews in Queen Isabella's Spain in order to get their wealth for Spain's American empire-building, developed cruelty to an art that left Heydrich and Eichmann little to add.

Inquisitional tortures continued well into the eighteenth century.

Neither illness nor pregnancy could spare a woman from the bite of the Inquisition instruments wielded by the protectors of loving Christ. Since all the property of the convicted fell to the Inquisition corporation, to be shared equally by their majesties, there was an added incentive to intensify the Inquisition. Denouncers were well rewarded, and a person denounced was a person indicted and convicted, since no living creature could withstand the refined methods of punishment the clerics had devised. Every single part of the human anatomy had been carefully studied and experimented upon to find those most sensitive to pain.

Scarcely ever since has excruciating maltreatment been refined as it was by the Dominicans and other practitioners of the Holy Office of the Inquisition.

Gui's manual tells the Inquisition staff and their spies how to discover "Jewish practices" among "converts" and Marranos:

"Putting on clean or festive clothes, clean and washed shirts and hairdress; arranging and cleaning their house on Friday afternoon, and in the evening lighting new candles, with new tapers and torches, earlier than on other days of the week; cooking on the said Fridays such food as is required for the Saturday, and on the latter eating the meat thus cooked on the Friday, as is the manner of the Jews; keeping the Jewish fasts, not touching food the whole day until nightfall, and especially the Fast of

Queen Esther, and the chief fast of Cinquepur (Yom Kippur), and other Jewish fasts, laid down by their law . . . and on the said fast days asking pardon of one another in the Jewish manner, the younger ones to the elder, the latter placing their hands on the heads of the former, but without signing them with the sign of the cross . . . Saying Jewish prayers . . . with the face turned to the wall, moving the head backwards and forwards as the Jews do; cutting the nails and keeping, burning or burying the parings; cleaning or causing meat to be cleaned, cutting away from it all fat and grease, and cutting away the nerve of the sinew of the leg . . . killing oxen as the Jews do, covering the blood with cinders or with earth; giving the Jewish blessing before eating, called the *baraha;* reciting words over the cup or vase of wine, after which each person sips a little, according to the custom of the Jews; not eating pork, hare, rabbit, strangled birds, conger-eel, cuttle fish, nor eels or other scaleless fish, as laid down in Jewish law . . . pouring water from jars and pitchers when someone has died . . . making divinations for children born to them, on the seventh day; not baptizing them, and when they have been baptized scraping off the Chrism put on them in the sacrament of baptism. . . . If they give Old Testament names to the children, or bless them by the laying of hands; if women do not attend church within forty days after confinement; if the dying turn towards the wall; if they wash a corpse with warm water; if they recite the Psalms without adding the *Gloria Patri* at the close; who say that the dead Law of Moses is good, and can bring about their salvation, and perform other rites and ceremonies of the same."

GUILDS

of craftsmen throughout the Christian territories of Europe up to the eighteenth century rejected Jews as members. If any Jewish craftsman succeeded in joining a local unit, the other members relentlessly pressured for his expulsion. The Church-based anti-Semitic homiletics had taken their effect.

In the earlier years of Hitlerism the Catholic and Protestant exclusion tactics were adopted by the Nazified guilds and societies and all Jews were expelled. The expellees, of course, were later systematically executed; the persecution of Jews by the churches in previous centuries, while equally hateful, was less efficient.

GUILT

Hitler finding the Jews guilty of Germany's defeat in the First World War is the same as the Bishop of Orleans blaming the Jews for the destruction of the Church of the Holy Sepulcher in Jerusalem, or the Bishop of Rome condemning the Jews for an earthquake that disturbed the Easter procession in 1020.

Jew hatred has its own logic.

GUILT (COLLECTIVE)

During the slave revolt of August, 1791, in Santo Domingo, mobs of Negroes carried a giant crucifix through the streets, howling:"The whites have killed Jesus! Kill all the whites!" This ironic parallel to the Church's blanket indictment of the Jews was recorded by Heinrich Heine.

GUILT BY RELATION

is a variation of the judicial malpractice of guilt by association. During the McCarthy era in the United States thinking people, Protestants and Catholics alike, abhorred the idea that a man might be punished because his brother was an alleged or proven defector, or a woman subjected to criminal investigation because her mother was suspect.

It is astonishing to see the very same Catholic or Protestant theologians, teachers and clerics, who vociferously protested "guilt by relation" as a perversion of justice, accept with equanimity the condemnation of the Jewish people as a whole because some few members of their race thousands of years ago allegedly voted for the execution of one of their clan.

H

HEIDAMAKS

Ukrainian mercenary bands under the leadership of Cossack hetmen who roved Eastern Europe in the seventeenth century. The priests of the Greek Orthodox Church relentlessly incited them to destroy the accursed enemies of Christ. It took little fresh indoctrination to convert the Cossacks into a snarling pack of Jew-hounds.

HEP! HEP!

Anti-Semitic riot slogan, first shouted by the Crusaders; derived from the initials of the Latin phrase, *Hierosylma est perdita* ("Jerusalem is lost"). The cry was taken over by Hitler's storm troopers.

HERDER, JOHANN GOTTFRIED VON (1744-1803)

German Protestant theologian, court preacher at Weimar; an inspiration to the philosophical and theological faculties of Hitler Germany, Herder spoke thus of the people of God:

"The Jew is a parasite growing on the branches of other nations."

"Together with Fichte and Hegel, he placed the crown of 'Chosen People' on the Teutonic Nation."

HERR

The Nazi practice never to address a Jew with the usual *Herr* (Mister) had its origin in the Papal Bull of

July 12, 1555, issued by Pope Paul IV (1555-1559) entitled *Nimis absurdum*, wherein it is distinctly prohibited for Jews to refer to any of their race as "Mister" (*Herr*). On April 10, 1566, Pope Pius V renewed all orders of this Bull with his own *Romanus Pontifex.*

HILARY OF POITIERS, SAINT (d. 367)

marked the Jews as a perverse people, forever accursed by God.

HIPPOLYTUS

Third-century exegete of Catholicism. Like the generality of Church Fathers, he attacked the Jews on all grounds and no ground. He gloated over their sufferings because "they" were descendants of a race that rejected the Lord. He became one of the schismatic Bishops of Rome.

HITLER'S BIRTHDAY

On Hitler's fiftieth birthday, April 20, 1939, Protestant and Catholic bishops of all but two dioceses in Germany urged the following prayer in pastoral letters to the faithful:
"Remember O Lord our Führer, whose secret wishes Thou knowest. Protect him with Thy inexhaustible kindness. Give him the victory of heaven for him and his folk." (*Katholische Monatsschrift,* May, 1939)

HOMO DIABOLICUS

Nowhere outside Hitler's salons and meeting halls was the Jew so often referred to as "diabolical" as in the Christian churches. Time and time again in the Gospels, in Church edicts, catechisms and literature, Judaism is depicted as devilish and Jews as the Devil's brood.
The language used by the early Church Fathers, and

later by the Popes, in referring to Jews, resembles in coarseness and brutality, the style of Streicher rather than Hitler.

From Pope Innocent III, throughout the history of the Vatican, the Torah was called "vomit." If a forcibly "converted" Jew "relapsed" into the faith of his ancestors, the faith of Jesus and Joseph, the solemn word from the Chair of St. Peter was: The dog returns to his vomit.

The most colorful gutter descriptions of the Jews, however, were offered by Martin Luther, who wanted the lot of them wiped off the face of the earth. Common decency forbids the repetition of Luther's barnyard black-humor in this book. Those interested can find it in Streicher's *Stürmer*, where Luther is often quoted word for word, dirt for dirt.

HORNED HAT

The Catholic Council of Vienna decreed in 1267 that all Jews had to wear horned hats (*pileum cornutum*) to indicate that they were the offspring of the Devil.

HOST DESECRATION

In 1215 Pope Innocent III declared the consecrated wafer offered in communion to be the real body of Christ (doctrine of transubstantiation). After this date nothing was easier than for the generally anti-Semitic Catholic clergy to claim that Jews had nailed, cut or otherwise defamed the holy wafer—which meant Christ Himself.

Underlying the "host desecration" phobia was the idea expressed by the renowned Catholic preacher, Berthold of Regensburg, that Christ *physically* was present in every wafer. The Jews, by mutilating a consecrated wafer, could therefore kill Christ again and again.

In 1243, at Berlin, all Jews of the suburb Bernau were burned for host desecration. In 1510 twenty-six Jews were burned alive for piercing the Eucharist.

HUGH OF LINCOLN

In the year 1255, an English boy of that name was found dead in a well. Scores of Jews were apprehended and under unspeakable tortures all confessed to having crucified the child.

Such ritual murder trials were monstrosities, yet the Catholic Church has publicly denounced only the one held in the Italian city of Trent.

HUSSITES

Followers of the reforming Czech priest, John Huss (1369-1415). The Mother Church began its bloody war against them, as it did its similar campaigns against the Albigensians, Waldensians and other "heretics," with a massacre of Jews. This was an obvious political maneuver on the part of the Church to identify their current religious enemy with the traditional Devil's offspring, the Jew.

Hitler similarly accused the Communists, the Americans —indeed, all his adversaries—of being inspired, directed or allied with Jews.

HYMN BOOKS

"God has built His Church in spite of envious Jews." This is a quote offered by the great essayist Oliver Wendell Holmes in discussing the evil of anti-Semitic phrases in Protestant liturgy.

Holmes suggested the removal of all such offensive lines from Hymns, prayers and catechisms, since their repetition creates in the worshiper's mind a pattern of the Jew as an accursed killer.

An example taken from *The Child's Scripture* (Presbyterian) used in Sunday schools:

Question: "Who put Jesus to death?" Answer: "The wicked Jews."

93

Question: "How did they put him to death?" Answer: "On the cross."

The effect, of course, of such "teachings" on the child's soul is traumatic.

I

IGNATIEV, NIKOLAI PAVLOVICH (b. 1832)

Author of the notorious "May Laws" of Russia promoting anti-Semitic legislation. Direct organizer of pogroms by his "barefoot brigades." The Orthodox clergy were his most ardent collaborators.

IGNATUS III

Jacobite Patriarch, who declared in November, 1965: "It is a dogma of the Church that the guilt of the crucifixion of Christ must fall upon the Jews to the end of the world."

It appears that Pope Paul VI agrees, to judge by his outburst in March of that year, in which he scorned *the* Jews for "killing the Lord."

IMPRIMATUR BY THE VATICAN

Recently The Church published a new catechism for distribution to the school children in Italy. The Pope himself gave it his personal imprimatur. This book, which the present Pope endorsed, is entitled "Message of the Gospel." ("Il Messaggia Degli Evangli.") The author is Professor Don Angeli Alberti. Quoting from the text: "How much shame the Jews must feel when they see that The Devil, whom they prefer as their Leader, is defeated. And the Jews, like The Devil, will forever crawl round the world, defeated—reduced to a society of money-grubbers. God's Curse is reserved exclusively for them, and they will forever wander the earth. This is their Eternal Punishment for refusing to accept Jesus Christ."

INDIVIDUOS DE LA CALLE

Ghetto people of Palma on the island of Majorca, also known as "Chuetas." They are descendants of Jewish converts, Marranos, who ate pork in public to prove their Catholic faith. In 1591 more than fifty of them who tried to escape from the island were caught and burned at the stake.

The local Dominican monastery published in 1755 a complete list of Chuetas condemned to the "purifying flames."

The Chuetas are still pariah among the pure-blooded Catholics, who will neither associate nor intermarry with them.

INNOCENT III (1161-1216)

This most cruel of the cruel Popes threatened Alfonso the Noble of Castile with excommunication if he continued to treat the Jews like people. The gentle Vicar wrote: "The Jewish vagabonds are to be treated as serfs."

INSOLENCE

A repeated charge made by clerics against the Jews. Wherever and whenever secular authorities found room for the Jew in government or official enterprise, the ecclesiastics would raise a spiteful cry: "Insolence!"

The Church could not rest with a Jew in office anywhere. In 1081 Pope Gregory VII wrote to Alphonso VI of Castile: "We must warn Your Highness that the Crown cease to permit Jews to rule over Christians. To permit Jews to have authority over Christians is the same as to oppress the Church and elevate the synagogue."

INTIMACY

From the early Church Fathers to the end of the Papal States in 1870 the faithful were ordered by the hierarchy to avoid any intimacy or social intercourse with the Jews. In the March, 1936, No. 10, issue of *Der Stürmer,* Julius Streicher severely reprimanded a member of the Nazi party for having called a Jew his friend: "A German who fraternizes with a Jew is calling the Devil his brother." Streicher was only quoting from the *Bullum Romanum.*

ISIDOR OF SEVILLE, SAINT (560-636)

He, too, wrote a tract *Contra Judaeos.* It seems that all the loving saints of the first Christian millennium had an uncontrollable urge to say something nasty about the Jews. Insecurity? Fear of a vigorous rival faith? Rejection of their spiritual parents? A fawning need to absolve their adopted father, the Roman Emperor? Perhaps we should leave the question to the practitioners of pathological psychology.

J

JEROME, SAINT (d. 420)

Translator of the Vulgata, who proves in his *Tractate Against the Jews* that they are congenital liars who lure Christians into heresy. They should therefore be punished until they confess. With Saint Augustine he can be called the spiritual father of the Inquisition.

JESUITS

In their periodical, *Voce della Verità,* the Jesuits in 1873 forecast: "In case of reconciliation between the Pope and the Kingdom of Italy, the Jews will have to return to the ghetto."

Jesuits were the most anti-Semitic segment of the Polish clergy in the seventeenth century. Until quite recently, they also excluded all Catholics of Jewish blood from their society—a racialism practiced far more widely in Catholic circles than is generally known. The similarity to notorious modern racist ideologies is inescapable.

96

JESUS

While living on earth not only was He a Jew, He was the Jew of Jews, faithful to the Law of Moses, which, as He said, He came to fulfill, not to destroy. Without the Law of Moses, there could be no Christ, no Messiah. Jesus was circumcized, wore the long-falling earlocks of the Hebrews, keeping His hair uncut at the corners, would touch no flesh of the pig, would fast on the day of repentance, would eat no leavened bread at Passover time, would wash His hands before partaking of food while murmuring the prescribed blessing, would wear the ritualistic garment adorned with Tzitzin.

Jesus was a Jew among Jews, yet so has the Christian Gospel twisted truth and history that most of its readers identify only Judas with the Jews and Jesus with the "Gentiles," whatever that may mean, since neither Greeks nor Romans, Persians nor Syrians, expected a Messiah; and Jesus could neither speak in their alien tongues nor pray in accord with their alien paganisms.

When Jesus spoke, only Hebrews could and would listen; when he sent out His Apostles, only Jews were selected; and when He gave up His Soul, it were daughters of Israel who wept for Him.

JEW

Hitler used only the singular for the Jewish people, never the plural. Whatever displeased him he would blame on *"Der Jud."*

Nazis referred to "the banker Jew," although of the nine million Jews of Europe, six million lived in the slums of Russia, Poland and the Balkans, many existing from hand to mouth in an almost beggarly manner.

The Christian Gospels and theologians similarly refer always to "the Jews" as a generalization, a generic term. They do not say some Jews voted against Jesus; they say "the Jews."

97

The Christian theologians call "the Jews" killers of Christ. although only a few hundred could possibly have voted before Pilatus to find Jesus guilty; most of the Jews in Palestine could not even have known of whatever trial there may have been, while the majority of Jews had long before left their homeland for Alexandria, Babylon, Rome and other cities.

Yet such is the nature of Christian "reasoning" that their theologians, like Hitler, hold all Jews responsible for what one or a few of them might have done thousands of years ago.

It was all the easier for Hitler to sway the Christian Germans and Austrians and much of the rest of Catholic Europe to his anti-Semitic philosophy because the Christians of Europe had for thousands of years been Church-trained to hold all Jews guilty of the failings of even one.

Church anti-Semitism fitted Nazi anti-Semitism hand in glove; as Hitler said, "I am only continuing the work of the Catholic Church in my fight against the Jews."

JEWISH DOCTORS

"Avoid seeking a Jewish physician and take no remedy from Jewish chemists." Time and time again did the Vatican repeat this admonition coupled with threats of severe punishment.

In 1934 the devout Christian, Julius Streicher, Gauleiter of Nuremberg, proclaimed: "Avoid the pernicious teachings of Pasteur, 'Judenstämmling.' Avoid the charlatan Robert Koch and his nefarious tuberculin. Avoid Paul Ehrlich, the Jew, and his Salvarsan; he drove millions of Germans to certain death in order to enrich himself."

Streicher only elaborated on the old Catholic edict. He also repeated the warning against Jewish doctors having intimacy with Christian virgins.

For a Protestant precedent in the identical vein, listen to Martin Luther, shortly before his death: "The Jews revile our Lord every day. If they had the power, they would kill us all. Indeed, their physicians often do it." Five hundred years later Josef Stalin, a theology seminarian of the Orthodox school, repeated the charge against Jewish doctors in Soviet Russia.

JEWISH MATERIALISM

In 1592 Pope Clement VIII wrote: "The world suffers from Jewish monopolies and their deceitful actions. The Jews have caused poverty especially to farmers and working-class people and the very poor."

The grammar is faulty even in the original Latin, but the text is a ready model for *Mein Kampf*. And, for a more recent reminder, the Nazi theorists had only to consult the encyclicals of Pope Leo XIII (*Tametsi*, 1900) and Pope Pius XI (*Quas Primas*, 1925) which warned the Christian world against "Jewish materialism."

JEWISH WORLD CONSPIRACY

The myth of the above, culminating in the long uncovered forgery, "The Protocols of Zion," was nourished by the Catholic hierarchy beginning in the early medieval centuries. In its more modern form it appears in the "Mémoire pour servir à l'histoire du Jacobinisme" by the French Jesuit, the Abbé Barruel in 1797.

Barruel describes the French Revolution as the planned culmination of secret societies directly inspired by the devilish Jews. In similar manner of reasoning Streicher traced the origin of Communism to Jewish planning of world conquest. Both the Catholic Church and the National Socialist Party condemn Freemasonry, an offshoot of French Revolutionary thinking, as a creation of Jewish planning to undermine "Christian" morality. To the Catholic Church even today Masonry is anathema and off limits on pain of excommunication. To Abbé Barruel the sinister head of the

99

conspiracy was Adam Weishaupt, a Bavarian Jew, one of the "Sons of Satan."

In 1806 Abbé Barruel presented to influential circles in Catholic France a letter allegedly received from an army officer, J. B. Simonini, whose identity the Abbé failed to establish, claiming to "have knowledge" that the Jews had already established cells in all towns and villages of Christian Europe in order to take over the western world including the Catholic Church. All churches would be turned into synagogues and all Christians reduced to slavery.

The Holy Synod of the Orthodox Russian Church jumped into the fray stamping Napoleon Bonaparte as the Anti-Christ, since he offered the Jews of Europe the civil rights they were utterly deprived of by the Christian churches (October 1806, Moscow).

Together with a fellow Jesuit, Father Grivel, Barruel wrote expanding papers on the structure of the Secret International whose Jewish Grand Master "had power over life and death of all Freemasons, including members of the Inner Council." "The purpose of this world-wide conspiracy is the creation of revolutions, upheavals, unrest and assassinations."

It almost seems that Hitler took whole paragraphs of his "Mein Kampf" from the zealous Jesuits.

The French Catholic Gougenot des Mousseaux belabored at great length the issue of Jewish-Freemasonry Conspiracy in his anti-Semitic text "Le Juif, le Judaisme et la judaisation des peuples chrétiens" (Paris, 1869). His book, widely publicized by the Hitler elite, had been enthusiastically prefaced by the head of the Foreign Missions Catholic Seminary in Paris, and the author received special blessings by Pope Pius IX for his Christian coinage.

An epigone of both Barruel and Mousseaux was the Abbé Chabauty, curé of Saint-André at Mirebeau in Poitou.

In his work "Les France-Macons et les Juifs" he reasoned that Satan himself masterminded the Jewish-Masonic plot to dominate the world.

100

"The Protocols of Zion," forgeries from Alpha to Omega, the last chapter in the anti-Semitic phantasy of the Christian Jew-baiters, at this writing is distributed in all Catholic republics of Latin America with headquarters in Mexico City. Even in New York City and Miami Beach the "book" enjoys unrestricted sales in foreign language and "Spanish" liturgical shops.

In the eighties of the last century Pope Leo XIII himself deemed it not below his dignity to encourage attacks against the Jews as Masonic conspirators. Father R. Ballerini and Father F. S. Rondina, affiliated with the Jesuit "La civiltà cattolica," depicted the Jews much in the manner of Streicher, as a giant octopus holding the Christian world in their grip.

Catholic papers throughout Europe called for a repeal of Jewish emancipation and sequestering of Jewish holdings.

It is such an arena that Hitler stepped into a generation later; the ground was well prepared, by the Christian churches of all denominations.

No adventurer was reckless enough, no schemer low enough, no politician cheap enough not to find support of the Christian churches in their effort to malign, vilify or slander the Jews. The Jew was *vogelfrei*, outside the protection of the law.

In 1893, in his book "La Franc-Maçonnerie, Synagogue de Satan" Monsignor Meurin, Archbishop of Port-Louis, Mauritius, declared that all Freemasonry was Jewish, exclusively Jewish. The bishop's congenial Léo Taxil, a sage to the French village priests, confided that the American Freemasons had a central telephone in New York operated by the Devil himself, who keeps in touch with his subordinates in this manner.

The Archbishop called on all rulers of the world to remove the Jews from places of writing, banking, teaching, medicine and all other communications in order to save the Church.

Hitler abided by this call, and the European Churches abided by Hitler.

JEWS' ISLE

Not until the middle of the eighteenth century did the clergy of Switzerland permit the Jews to bury their dead in Swiss soil. The Jews had to use as their burial ground a little river island beyond the borders.

JOHN I

King of England who in 1210 arrested all Jews in his domain and "fined" them whatever they possessed. Since Abraham of Bristol was unable to satisfy the greed of the King and his prelates, his teeth were pulled out one at a time.

JOHN XXII (1316-1334)

By far the wealthiest man of his time, this Pope was a far-planning financial genius. Simony within the church was so great that it became the focal point of Protestant attack. Yet the high clergy of this very era accused the Jews of being money-minded.

A prototype of the twentieth-century steel magnates and bank-Junkers of Germany, who joined the Nazi outcry against Jewish greed.

JOHN XXIII (1881-1963)

The one and only Pope ever to speak out in behalf of the Jews had, before his death, composed a *Prayer of Repentance* in which this true vicar of Christ begged God's forgiveness for the untold suffering brought upon the Jewish nation by the members of the Catholic Church. On his deathbed the Pontiff urged that this prayer be said in all Catholic places of worship. Up to now, this has not been done; the good Pope's wish should be neglected no longer.

Quoting from Pope John's *Prayer of Repentance*:

"We admit that over hundreds of years our eyes were blinded, so as not to see the Beauty of Thy Chosen People and not to recognize the features of our firstborn brother. We admit that the sign of Cain is upon our forehead. For centuries Abel was lying in blood and tears while we had forgotten Thy love. Forgive us, O Lord, the curse we unjustly spoke out over the people of Israel. Forgive us, that in their flesh we crucified You the second time! We did not know what we were doing. . . ."

JOHN, GOSPEL OF

is the most anti-Semitic Gospel of the four. It calls the Jews children of the Devil (VIII:44). Here are some other quotes from this tract of spiritual love:

"The Jews kept persecuting Jesus." (V:16)

"The Jews kept murmuring about Him." (VI:41)

"Jesus did not want to go to Judea because the Jews were seeking to put Him to death." (VII:1)

"Jesus asked the Jews, Why do you wish to kill me?" (VII:20)

"You children of Abraham are desirous of murdering me." (VIII:40)

"The Jews picked up stones to throw at Jesus, but He hid." (VIII:59)

"The Jews decided anybody who would accept Jesus would be expelled from the Synagogue." (IX:22)

"The Jews went out to seize Him but Jesus slipped through their hands." (X:39)

"Jesus did not dare to walk about openly; He withdrew with His disciples near the desert." (XI:54).

"The High Priests planned to kill Lazarus because he made others believe in Jesus." (XII:9)

"The Roman cohorts and the Jewish guards of the High Priest took Jesus into custody and bound Him." (XVIII:12)

"Jesus said: I might not be delivered to the Jews." (XVIII:36)

"Pilatus told the Jews again and again, Jesus is innocent. But the Jews cried: Do not set Him free." (XVIII: 38-40)

"Pilatus went out again where the Jews were and said: Jesus is innocent. But the High Priests and their guards cried out: Crucify Him!" (XIX:4-6)

"Pilatus was looking for a way to release Jesus, but the Jews shouted: If you release Jesus you are not loyal to Caesar." (XIX:12)

"Pilatus hesitated: Shall I crucify your King? And the High Priests answered: We have no King but Caesar." (XIX:15)

"The Jews pleaded with Pilatus to break the legs of the dying Jesus to hasten his death." (XIX:31)

"The disciples of Jesus gathered behind closed doors in fear of the Jews." (XX:19)

The above are verbatim quotations from the Gospel of St. John as it is taught to Christian children and adults in the Western world. Thus the scribes of the Bishops of Rome turned the simple Gospels of the Hebrew—and only—followers of the living Jesus into a totally perverted historiographic document that was designed to absolve the Caesars and their governors from all responsibility in the thousandfold massacres of the witnesses of Christ—to make these masters of the bloody coliseum charitable judges and to stamp the Jewish victims—of whom Jesus was just another example—as perpetrators of deicide.

Racial Christianity as practiced in Nazi Germany had its origins deep in the Gospel of St. John. This particular Gospel, more than the Synoptics, creates the impression that Christianity found its first followers among people fundamentally different from the Jews.

Jesus, His family and His friends are referred to as if they were gentiles, alien and inimical to the Jews, who are lurking in the background, ready and eager to destroy them. Concurrently, all mention of the Hebrews is defamatory and hostile: The Jews have no knowledge of God (8:19); The

104

Jews are imitators of the Devil, who is their father (8:44); The Jews are forever in sin and are doomed to die thus (8:21).

No wonder that among unbiased Christian historians, as well as Jewish scholars, the Evangelist John is known as "the father of anti-Semitism."

Not once—but not once—does the word "Jew" appear in the Gospel of St. John except in derisive manner. The Gospel has without question served as a foundation of Jew hatred and contempt throughout the Middle Ages right up to the days of Streicher, who never tired of quoting from "his Bible."

To cleanse this Gospel of its malevolence would be a service not only to Jews in the modern community but also to the consciences of all liberal-minded Christians.

JOHN OF DIRPHEIM

This Bishop of Strasbourg demanded and received from King Henry VII of Germany in 1308 the Jews of Rufach and Sulzmatt. A few were thrown into dungeons, the majority burned alive. The charge was "desecrating" holy wafers.

In 1338 another group of Jews was massacred by the Bishop on the anniversary of the conversion of St. Paul.

JOHN OF EPHESUS (516-585)

claimed the honor of having destroyed seven Jewish temples and turned them into churches, an example that guided Christian rulers for a thousand years. The destruction of synagogues was carried to its ultimate on November 10, 1938, when the Nazis destroyed all Jewish houses of worship in Germany and Austria.

JUDAS

A device of the Roman Gospel writers to stamp Iscariot, the alleged betrayer of Jesus with the surname of "Judean" (Jew).

As Pope Gelasius I (492-496) philosophized: "In the Bible the whole is often named after the part; as Judas was called a devil and the devil's workman, he gives his name to the whole race."

In similar vein, modern anti-Semites stigmatize one Jew and involve the whole nation as his identicals. Rothschild is a capitalist—all Jews are capitalists. Trotsky is a Communist—all Jews are Communists.

Recent sociological polls show that almost half of the Catholics in this country believe Judas, the traitor, was a Jew and that barely ten per cent realize that all the Apostles of Christ were Jews. Only five per cent of the Catholics were aware that St. Paul was actually Saul, a Jewish rabbinical student.

All without exception considered the Catholic faithful as having taken the divine prerogative of being "God's Chosen People."

JUDE

This German word for Jew became a term of opprobrium, especially in the Hitler era.

Here, again, the German Nazis harked back to the hissing hate of the early Church Fathers.

Eusebius of Caesarea, the Church historian, used the term "Jew" only in reproach or derogation, as did Justin Martyr, Clement of Alexandria, Origen of Caesarea, Ephraem, Jerome, Augustinus, etc.

106

JUDENBLICK

was introduced into the German language by wandering monks as a synonym for "evil eye." A favorite expression of Streicher.

JUDEN-NASE

or "Jew-nose," mocking German reference to Jews as characterized by hooked or bent noses; widely used by Nazi propagandists, it originated in the church decoration and liturgical illustrations of medieval Catholicism.

Medieval religious art abounds with examples. To mention only a few—

—In the Berner Chronicle of 1474-1483, Picture No. 13 depicts Jewish ritual murderers (*Kindfresser*) with *"Krumme Nasen";*

—The Florentine Chronicle of Giovanni Villani marks the Jewish "torturer" of a blessed wafer with an exaggerated nose;

—A French chronicle of 1321, illustrating the expulsion of the Jews by Philip Augustus, shows his victims with ugly bent noses;

—In the Rhein Codex Balduini of 1330 the leader of a Jewish deputation seeking audience with Heinrich VII appears endowed with a *Juden-Nase* that would have done credit to *Der Stürmer.*

The origin of most such Nazi Antisemitica can easily be traced to medieval Christian liturgy and art in which the Jew is portrayed not only as spiritually deformed, but as a physically ugly monster.

The medieval horned hat forced upon Jews derives from the gospel reference to Hebrews as Devil's offspring. Conversely, the Devil is often depicted in medieval church art with "Jewish" attributes, such as a hooked nose, Star-of-David badge, and the like.

JUDENREIN

"Clean of Jews." This term, widely used in the Hitler era, was coined in the middle of the fourteenth century in Germany by the Catholic clergy, who incited the faithful to exterminate the Sons of the Devil on the charge of well poisoning. Within two years nearly 350 Jewish communities were tortured into confessions and then "drowned, burned, hanged or burned alive," as contemporary chronicles report.

Germany was *"judenrein,"* to be made so once again by German Christians raised on the same hate theology.

Hans Frank, the infamous Nazi Governor of Poland, stated on August 1, 1942, in Cracow: "No Jew will ever see Germany." Similar statements were uttered scores of times by bishops, cardinals and popes alike when they expelled or martyred Jews in France, England, Spain and Portugal.

JUDENSAU

"Jew Pig," a cartoon-symbol of a pig giving milk to piglets and Jews which decorates choir stalls, pillars and eaves of Protestant churches in Wittenberg, Regensburg, Basel and elsewhere.

In the cathedral of Wittenberg a rabbi stands behind the sow, holding up its tail. As Luther describes this bit of art: "The Rabbi looks into—the Talmud."

Streicher reproduced some of these examples of religious aesthetics.

JUDENSTEIN

This rock in Rinn, Austria, where allegedly on July 12, 1462, Jews murdered a Christian child to drink its blood, was until recently visited by devout pilgrims who promised themselves miracles. An ugly anti-Semitic reference had been engraved there by the Church.

JUDENZOLL

"Cattle tax" imposed upon Jews in Central Europe when traveling from one town to another. Existed up to the eighteenth century.

Toll charges were often designed to humiliate the Jew. Philip V, the Catholic monarch of Spain (1703), fixed the toll at one head of cattle for one Jew. In other places Jews were ordered to cast dice as a reminder of Golgotha, though even the Gospels record that it was Pilate's Roman soldiers who gambled for Jesus' raiment. In most Christian countries the Jews had to pay a head tax.

In Salzburg the Catholic Bishop retained the Jew tax until 1791. As elsewhere, the change was brought by the French Revolution, whose adherents considered the cattle taxes abhorrent and inhuman.

JUSTINIAN'S CODE—See *Corpus Juris Civilis*

JUSTITIA ET MISERICORDIA

"Justice and Charity" was the inscription on the banners of the Inquisition. The chief question which concerned the charitable judges of holy law was whether the convicted should die by fire. Guilt could always be proven by torture.

The question has never been answered: Which was the deeper motivation of these heartless holy men—greed for the property of the condemned, or religious fanaticism?

K

KATHOLISCHE JUGENDGRUPPE

This nationwide Catholic youth organization of Germany was combined with the Hitler *Jungvolk* following the Concordat of Collaboration sponsored by Msgr. Pacelli, later Pope Pius XII. Together, they sang the *Horstwessel Lied* in the church vestries: *"Wenn das Judenblut vom Messer spritzed . . ."* (When the blood of the Jews runs off the dagger).

KINDFRESSERBRUNNEN

The "fountain of the child devourer," erected in 1540 in Bern, depicting a Jew with a sackful of infants and swallowing one of them. In 1294 all Jews of this Swiss town were either killed or expelled because of an alleged "ritual murder."

KISHINEV

City in Bessarabia; while under Czarist Russian rule, scene of a severe pogrom in April, 1903, which began with a Church-inspired ritual murder accusation. Orthodox seminarians had a heavy hand in the murder of the Jews.

Under Soviet rule the traditional attitude toward the Jew is maintained: F. Mayatsky, author of the anti-Semitic tract *Contemporary Judaism and Zionism* in 1965 was appointed full professor of philosophy at the State University of Kishinev.

KREMS

A town in Austria where, in 1349, all Jews were driven into their houses and burned alive on the charge of having brought the Asian plague. Similar outrages were committed in Germany and Switzerland by a population incited to Jew hatred by a fanatical Christian clergy.

L

LA CIVILTA CATTOLICA

Official Jesuit journal, published in Rome, which supported with vehemence the anti-Semitic attacks on Alfred Dreyfus, even after his innocence was proven in the French military courts. Agreeing with Bismarck's statement that "The Jews were created by God to act as spies," the journal suggests that Jews be deprived of citizenship and remain in the land only as "alien guests."

A generation later, in 1936, *Civiltà Cattolica* took the same medieval stance in an article on Nazi anti-Semitism. The editor explained that the Christian world (Germany) must defend itself ("without unchristian hate of course") against the Jewish danger by withdrawing all civil rights from Jews and placing them in ghettos.

LA CROIX

Daily French paper edited and published by the Fathers of the Assumption during the latter part of the nineteenth century, which supported strenuously the anti-Semitic journalism of Edouard Drumont, most vicious Jew baiter of France.

Like Hitler, Drumont maintained proudly, "I am guarding the Christian world against the Jews. I am defending the creation of the Lord."

The clergy of France stood behind Drumont, as the clergy of Germany stood behind Hitler. *Le Monde,* the unofficial organ of the French Catholic hierarchy, put itself completely at the disposal of Drumont. Monsignor d'Hulst introduced Drumont as "Sergeant of Christ."

In another paper, *L'Univers* (May, 1886), a missionary priest interpreted Drumontism as the "expropriation of Jewish property." Here, too, Hitler found a page to borrow from Catholic text.

LAGARDE, PAUL ANTON DE (1827-1891)

Prominent German Protestant theologian of Göttingen, specializing in ethics, who referred to the Jews as fungus. This influential teacher of Protestant seminarians rejected the "humanist" idea of dealing with the Jews as people. "They are *Bacillen* and should be exterminated, not saved."

111

A few generations later, Hitler used the very same term concerning the Jews—*"Bacillen"*—and the many Protestant students of Lagarde kept a reverent silence when the extermination began.

LAMENNAIS, FELICITE ROBERT DE (1782-1854)

French priest and social philosopher who considered the Jews lower than slaves: "Indeed, even slaves have to stoop in order to see them."

Such an assertion, of course, only repeated the beliefs of the early Church Fathers, but this was written after the French Revolution. The Nazi Alfred Rosenberg shared Lamennais' "thinking."

LAND

The refusal to sell land to a Jew has been for fifteen hundred years official policy of the Church. As late as 1893 the Catholic Diet of Cracow (Poland) declared: The Jews are our enemies; who sells a piece of land to a Jew or leases it to him is undermining the welfare of our nation. A generation later Hitler incorporated this stricture in his Nazi platform.

No state is more devotedly dedicated to agriculture than Israel, yet for centuries the Christian clergy, from Martin Luther and Saint (!) Vincente Ferrer of Inquisition fame, repeated the fatuous charge that Jews refused to work the land.

To begin with, except in the free States of America, up to the late eighteenth century the tillers of the Christian world were little more than serfs, villeins or slaves. In Russia they remained so until 1861. Furthermore, the Christian churches had, since the days of the Jew-hating Church Fathers, constantly exhorted, admonished, and ukased both Christian land-owners and serfs to shun association with Jews.

Thirdly, the Jew could hardly acquire land in Christian

Europe where, as late as 1869, countries such as Switzerland, northern Italy, Bavaria, and Prussia refused to grant him civil rights and permanent residence. The Jew, therefore, had to resort to artisanship and other professions which he could ply while on the run. The Germans referred to the Jews as *Packjuden* because the Jews carried packs on their shoulders like the Wandering Jew, Ahasuerus, of medieval legend. The Jew was the gypsy of Christian Europe, forever on the run, driven out of one town, looking for work in the next. Many towns limited his stay to months, weeks or even days. And behind this unrelenting pressure from his Church-inspired Christian neighbors was the threat of another horrible pogrom.

So the Jew of the Middle Ages became an artisan or petty trader in the service of villages or small cities, living his fearful ghetto existence at the end of town. The Jew was often the poorest of the poor, but the churches managed, as did the Nazis later with the fictional Süss, to build up a singularly wealthy Jew as the prototype of all Jews.

Hitler successfully inflated the canard of Jewish capitalism to fantastic proportions, although of the nine million Jews of pre-war Europe, nine-tenths lived from hand to mouth in pogrom-ridden Eastern Europe.

It was easy for Hitler; the Church had portrayed the Jews for centuries in the Gospel image of "moneychangers."

LAODICEA, COUNCIL OF

Fourth-century assembly of church leaders; forbade Christians to respect the Jewish Sabbath.

LEO VII

This good Pope of the tenth century suggested that the Jews be given the Gospel to hear, and if they rejected it, that they be expelled.

LES JUIFS DEVANT L'EGLISE ET L'HISTOIRE

In this standard work of the Dominican doctor of canonical law, Pater Constant (1897), the following is stated about the Jews:

"In the heart of every Jew flows a traitor's blood."

"A Jewish child over the age of seven can be baptized against its parents' will."

"No Christian may be in the service of a Jew."

"No Christian woman may nurse a Jewish infant; this would appear to the Church an outrage; it means bringing the Devil into contact with the Holy Ghost." [The Devil, of course, is the Jewish child.]

"A Christian may not eat with a Jew."

"Even in a prayer the Jew must be referred to as 'perfidious.'"

"A Jew may not instruct a Christian, in science or out."

"A Jew may not occupy a position of honor or a public office."

"A Jewish physician may not attend a sick Christian."

"A Jew may not be a magistrate because of his perfidy."

"A Jew may not be a soldier; he may only be an old clothes dealer, a ragman, a peddler or a moneylender."

So reads the treatise on justice of the distinguished Dominican, written at the turn of this century. Such, historically, are the wishes and often the ordinances of the Church in relation to the Jews. Modifications occur only insofar as the Church lacks power of enforcement. Was Hitler wrong in stating, "I am only continuing the work of the Catholic Church"?

LIMPIEZA DE SANGRE

Spanish term, meaning "purity of blood." Much of the time of the church functionaries of the Spanish Inquisition was taken up with examination of the racial background of the accused. Dissidents, heretics or suspects with even a trace of Jewish blood were foredoomed.

The concept of *limpieza* had begun to poison Spain before the Inquisition was established in 1478. In June, 1449, "Aryan" Catholics in the town of Villa Real fell upon the Semitic Christians (Marranos), mutilating and murdering the lot of them. They spared only those who could claim blood-pure Christian descent for three generations. Similar outrages occurred in the fourteenth and fifteenth centuries throughout Spain.

We note that Hitler's blood-purity rule, recognizing as Germans only "Aryan" people of the third generation, was clearly formulated by Catholic fanatics in Spain five hundred years before.

LONDON

In the early Middle Ages ecclesiastical pressure upon the Jews of England never ceased. Mobs were driven to riot, kings to confiscation.

In 1262 in the city of London fifteen hundred Jews were butchered. In 1279, 280 more were executed at the behest of the Catholic Church, and the rest driven from the city. Their possessions fell to the crown. In 1290 King Edward I, on All Saints' Day, ordered that all Jews be shipped out of his kingdom on hired boats. Perverse captains drowned many a Jew for his remaining belongings.

The early kings of England played a sinister game in collaboration with the bishops: The bishops got the Jews killed or exiled, the kings got their property.

LUBLIN

In this Polish city in 1648 Jesuits led a mob into the ghetto where they cut down eight Jews. For this pogrom they were publicly brought to account by King Ladislaus IV. Their influence, however, continued to make itself felt through anti-Semitic sermons and pamphlets. They were also responsible for the ban against Jews serving as pharmacists.

LUCERNE

From this Swiss city the Jews were expelled in 1401 by direct pressure from the Church and not permitted to settle again until 1869.

LUEGER, KARL (1844-1910)

Leading anti-Semitic politician of late nineteenth-century Austria, who propagated "Christian Socialism." As Mayor of Vienna, he was strongly supported by clerical elements. The rabble he roused from among the Austrian lower middle-class included an unknown young man named Adolf Hitler.

LUTHER, MARTIN (1481-1545)

This terrible man was a predecessor of Hitler. He demanded that all Jews not only become slaves, as Saint Augustine ordained, but be made slaves of the serfs, so they might never touch the hand of a Christian German.

In his tract *Schem Hamphoresh* (1544) Luther referred to the Jews as ritual murderers, poisoners of wells and, since they were worse than devils, demanded the burning of "all their synagogues and talmuds."

Here is what the foremost Protestant leader recommends for the Jews:

"They should be forced to hardest labor as handymen of serfs only; they should not be permitted to hold services; every Christian should be admonished to deal with them in a merciless manner; if you suffer, strike them in the jaw; if I had the power, I would assemble them to prove to us that we Christians do not worship God, under penalty of having their tongues cut out through the backs of their necks."

Luther's references to the Jews in his pamphlet *Die Juden und ihre Lügen* (*About the Jews and Their Lies*) are not repeatable. They are coarse, vile, vicious and vulgar.

Luther had spewed forth enough seed for the fresh growth of anti-Semitism in its most atrocious forms.

LWOW

In this Polish town severe persecution of the Jews commenced September 1, 1592 when Archbishop Salikowski ordered the Jews to erect a church. In rapid succession followed accusations of blood drinking and host desecration. In 1603 the Jesuits closed the synagogue. Only by paying heavy ransom could the Jews rededicate their temple in 1609.

LYON

Copies of tax records indicate that by order of the archbishop of this city (1340) a Jew who passed through Lyon had to pay 12 deniers as tariff or else receive a blow.

LYUTOSTANSKY, HIPPOLYTE

Catholic priest who was converted to the Russian Orthodox Church, and in 1869 distributed a booklet on *The Use of Christian Blood by Jews in Their Rituals*. He was one of the molders of the anti-Semitic mind of Czar Nicholas II.

M

MAGDEBURG

Archbishop Robert of this German city in 1261 seized all the property of "his" Jews and held the influential ones for ransom by "foreign" relatives.

An inspiration to Adolf Eichmann, who offered Jews for a ransom of trucks.

MAINZ

In this medieval trade center of the German Rhineland, hundreds of Jews were massacred by Crusaders infuriated by a fanatical Catholic clergy; only a few chose baptism before death.

MALA SANGRE

"Bad blood" was attributed to the Jews in fifteenth-century Spain by the Franciscan friar, Alphonso de Spina, in his book *Fortalitium Fidei*. He accused even the Marranos and conversos (converts) of being defiled forever by their Jewish blood. He appealed for a pure-blooded Christian Spain and the destruction of all racial Jews, professing or converted. His exhortations found willing listeners among the Catholic faithful. See *Limpieza de Sangre*.

MARIE THERESE (1717-1780)

Catholic Empress of Austria, strongly anti-Semitic, who decreed the yellow badge for Jews and endeavored to drive them from Bohemia.

MARRANOS

Spanish word meaning "pig," probably adapted from the Arabic word *mahram* which meant "something prohibited"; commonly used as a term for Jews or Moors who had been converted to Christianity, especially those suspected of accepting the Christian religion only to escape persecution. To prove their "sincerity," such converts might be called upon to eat pork in public.

Marranos were often treated by the Catholic authorities like common Jews who had to be obliterated. Hitler adopted the same attitude toward the European Catholics of Jewish origin. See also *Chueta*.

118

MARTINEZ, FERNANDO

was one of the Spanish Dominican friars who in 1369 exerted pressure on Henry II, King of Leon and Castile, to demand such exorbitant taxes of the Jews that many had to sell themselves into slavery in order to escape death by burning.

In his fanatical preaching Martinez "proved" that the Jews were responsible for the Black Plague because of their uncleanliness and malodor. (The latter charge often was repeated by Julius Streicher, arch-publicist of Nazi anti-Semitism!)

Martinez inflamed the populace of Seville into anti-Jewish riots. Jews were ordered into *juderías,* and the homes as well as the synagogues of the unfortunate were burned. (Here, too, the National Socialists of Germany followed the Catholic example: All synagogues were put to the torch by the German Neo-Inquisitionists.)

Martinez compelled the Hebrews to wear badges of recognition and forbade them to ride horseback. He prohibited sexual intercourse between Jews and Iberians, even prostitutes, and debarred them from all licensed professions. (Hitler emulated the Dominican, adopting all of his strictures, even the prohibition against riding horseback.)

The Dominicans, however, extended special leniency to Jewish children—if they informed on their parents. You can imagine the fate of the luckless parents!

MARX, KARL (1818-1883)

A childhood convert to Protestantism, he adopted Lutheran anti-Semitism. In his pamphlet, *Zur Judenfrage,* he charges that the basis of Judaism is greed; the Jew's God is money. Marx demanded the emancipation of the world from Jewish usury and money, a slogan readily taken over by Hitler.

119

MECKLENBURG

On October 24, 1492, twenty-four Jews, two of them women, were burned alive in this German city after a priest charged that they had impaled a consecrated wafer. The place of the pyre is still called *Judenberg*.

MEMORBUCH

A book to commemorate the names and events of the martyrdom of the Jewish people at the hands of the Christian clergy and their helpers.

MEXICO

From 1536 (the first auto-da-fé) until 1820 (close of the Holy Office) hundreds of Jews, Judaizers and Marranos were indicted and burned by the Catholic hierarchy.

The Catholic clergy in Mexico has written its own special chapter in anti-Semitism. Numerous Marranos were put to torture and "confessed," involving their own kin and friends. Francisca Nuñez de Carabajal was kept in dungeons for over three years, living from one excruciating torture to another, always in the presence of Catholic priests with Christ on their lips and venom in their hearts. She was finally burned alive on February 24, 1590. So monstrous was her agony during her confinement that she implicated her own children in fantastic evil deeds.

Even after a half-century of revolutionary secularization and disestablishment of the Catholic Church, Mexico City today is the source of thousands of copies of anti-Semitic works, including the infamous "Protocols of the Elders of Zion," reprinted in the Spanish language. These new bottlings of an old poison are widely distributed in Central and South America. Mysterious subsidies have brought more thousands of these works to bookstores in the United States which are patronized by Spanish-speaking Americans and Cuban refugees.

MISCEGENATION

The "Seven Part Code" of King Alfonso X (1252-1284) proposed by the Castilian clergy stipulated (Law IX): "Jews who have carnal relations with Christian women are guilty of criminal insolence and shall be put to death."

Hitler adopted this law for Germany.

Like the Church, however, Nazi Germany "tolerated" the "use" of Jewish women by Christians; in fact, the Nazi troops, who, let us recall, were blessed enthusiastically by both Protestant and Catholic clergy, had their military bordellos stocked with Jewish virgins taken from their families during the extermination roundup.

Many of the basic statutes of the Nuremberg Law can be found in the Code of the Roman Emperor Constantine I (306-337), who adopted the cross as a symbol of imperial rule. Constantine, who murdered his wife and son, ordained: No Jew may marry a Christian; no Jew may fraternize with a Christian; no Jew may hold an office reserved for Christians.

MONEYCHANGERS

The traditional identification of this Gospel reference with "*the* Jews"—as if the other attendants at the Temple were "Gentiles"—was frequently used by Hitler and Stalin. In one of his speeches Hitler compared himself to Jesus Christ and stated that like Him he would drive out the Jewish moneychangers, "a brood of vipers and adders from the temple of purity."

Indeed, no modern literature is as full of Gospel citations as that of the great anti-Semites of France, Germany, Spain and Russia.

121

The Gospel of St. John contains thirty-two references to "the Jews," all associating them with hateful actions from blood greed to sadism and foul betrayal.

The Gospel of St. John reads as if Jesus were living in a Gentile world, brutally interfered with by Jews, "whom He fled and avoided." How is the lay Christian to know that Jesus grew up in a Jewish home, observed all the rituals so often ridiculed by outsiders, spoke only Hebrew and its vernacular Aramaic, preached only to Jews in their synagogues or assemblies, was followed only by Hebrews, all his Apostles and those who loved Him and believed in Him being Jews?

The whole advent of Christianity was a Jewish drama, from alpha to omega, except the crucifixion, which was pure Roman. The Romans tolerated no king but Caesar, no God but Caesar.

It suited the Catholic Bishops of Rome, given supreme pontificate over the Empire, to show their gratitude to Emperor Constantine by "rehabilitating" the Roman police chief, the Procurator of Judaea, as a noble judge and blaming Jesus' agony on the ancestors of the obdurate Jews who would not bend their knees to the Bishop of Rome.

The Jews were the makers of Christianity, from Jesus to Paul, and not its destroyers.

MONGOLS

Their invasion of Eastern Europe in the Middle Ages was also blamed on the Jews by an ever eager clergy, claiming they were the "lost ten tribes of Israel," and that "the Jews are in league with the Mongols to kill the Christians as they killed Christ."

MONIEUX

A walled town in France near the Italian border where the armies of the First Crusade in 1095 put to death all Jewish inhabitants. A Hebrew chronicle of the day, set down by a Jewish woman who escaped as by a miracle, gives the details of this home-front heroism by the soldiers of the Cross, hundreds of miles from the Holy Land.

MONKS

and the lower Catholic clergy were among the worst inciters of anti-Semitic riots right up to the eighteenth century. Lack of substantial education left them little above the man of the plow or the man of the street. However, "the cloth" gave them enough protection and respect to allow them to rave and riot against "the killers of Christ."

In 1350 in the Bohemian town of Eger a "preaching monk" raised the mob and all Jews were massacred, their houses plundered, their books sent to the Bishop of Prague.

Similar incidents occurred a thousand times over in a Europe darkened by Catholicism for eighteen hundred years.

MORE JUDAICO

The Jewish oath was based upon the Christian church concept that Hebrews were, by definition, deceptors and enemies of truth. In practice, while the Church was dominant, the Jew's word was never taken against a Christian, and contrariwise, the Christian's oath on the New Testament was nearly always taken against a Jew.

The German Catholic Church authorities produced in the thirteenth century a widely popular form of Jewish oath: the Jew had to stand on the raw hide of a sow, facing an open Torah. He still was scarcely ever believed, of course, but the ceremony produced a double insult to the Jew, his faith, and his belief in his own dignity.

With the rise of worldly jurisprudence the Jewish oath became modified. The churches, however, while losing ground to the state jurists, retained their spiritual hold on both judges and juries, and the Jew avoided whenever possible the frustration of going to court against a Christian.

More judaico was abolished in Western Europe during the first half of the nineteenth century; in Rumania not until 1914.

MORTARA AFFAIR

As late as 1850 in Italy a bigot nurse secretly had a sickly Jewish infant baptized to "assure its recovery." In 1858 the Church authorities kidnaped the child and by order of Pope Pius IX refused to return it to its parents unless they themselves would convert. Three hundred years earlier this sort of crime was commonplace; in the nineteenth century it caused quite a stir in the Western world, but to no avail.

MOSCOW

Under Ivan III (1440-1505) a council of the Eastern Orthodox Church was convoked which accused Jews of slandering God's Son. A number of Jews were burned alive, others perished in the dungeons.

MOSLEMS

If not for the hospitality extended by Sultan Bayazid II of Turkey and other Moslem rulers, the Jews of Western and Southern Europe would have perished in the Inquisition era.

MUELLER, LUDWIG

On July 23, 1933, a group of National Socialist Protestant ministers, among whose "honorary" members were Frick and Göring, won a clear majority among the Lutheran clergy of Germany and elected Reverend Ludwig Mueller their *Reichsbischof*. Ludwig Mueller, a rabid anti-Semite, met Hitler in 1926. They compared their respective views most favorably.

MUFTI, THE

Haj Amin el-Husseini, Palestinian Arab leader, designated Mufti, or chief counselor in Koranic law, of Jerusalem during British rule of the Holy Land. Instigator of anti-Jewish demonstrations and riots; after outbreak of World War II, fled to Nazi Germany. There he endorsed Hitler's anti-Semitic program, his logic being that if the Jews were exterminated in Europe, there would be no further Jewish immigration to Palestine. He attempted to win recruits for Hitler's armies among the Moslem population of the occupied Balkan countries. Proclaimed a war criminal after Allied victory, he found refuge in Cairo, Egypt.

N

NANCY

The bishop of Nancy spoke at the French National Assembly in Paris on December 23, 1789: "The Christian people regard the Jews with abhorrence; to grant them rights as citizens would set all France aflame."

Adolf Hitler concurred a century and a half later, and one of his first deeds of statecraft was to abolish the civil rights of Jews.

NARBONNE

In 897 the bishop of this French town appropriated all the Jewish lands in his diocese with the help of the feeble King Charles the Simple. Appropriation of Jewish property has been widely practiced in our time by professional anti-Semitic governments.

NAZI VATICANISM

Despite all the enthusiastic ringing of church bells at Hitler visits, Hitler victory celebrations, *Dritte Reich* festivals, parties, and shows, I do not claim that all the Vatican hierarchy was Nazi-minded; but under Pope Pius XII the Vatican hoped for, fervently hoped for, Nazi victory and not that of the Allied cause.

In Rome itself the Pope, Pius XII, stood quietly at the window when Jewish women and children were seized at whip point and loaded into extermination buses.

There is one thing, however, that bothered the Vicar of Christ—namely, "What will become of Italy if the forces of Germany withdraw and we will be left at the mercy of the Allies? Freemasonry is already coming more and more to the fore!"

With great emotion the Pontiff then said:

"We empower you to state explicitly, to everyone, that the German people, in particular, have always been clasped in Our heart and that the German people, who are now being so sorely tried, are, more than any other nation, the object of Our very special concern. We have always given outward, as well as other, expression to our great sympathy for Germany, by interrupting Our private audiences so that members of the German Armed Forces who wished to visit Us might not have to wait unnecessarily.

"We make unceasing efforts to help, and especially to relieve the German people from the pressure of the dreadful terror attacks. Let everyone be convinced that, where the situation permits, we do everything that possibly can be done."

Even when Rome was in Allied hands, in 1944, the Germanophile Pope refused to raise even his voice in protest against the Himmler-Eichmann butchering of Hungarian Jews. He explained later, much later, that he did not want to give the thirty million Catholic Germans pangs of conscience about their wartime duties.

What nobility of motive lay behind his silence in the face of outrages committed on the children of the One Whose vicar he professed to be!

Following is an appeal of the cornered women, children and unarmed civilians of Jewish faith to the Catholic conscience:

"To the Christians of Hungary:

"In this final hour of their tragic destiny, the Jews of Hungary turn imploringly to the Christians of Hungary. They address their words to those whose existence they have shared for a thousand years, in good times and bad, on soil in which their ancestors are at rest.

"We kept silent when we were robbed of our possessions, when we lost our human dignity, and our status as citizens. We did not decide upon this extreme step even when we were driven from our homes. But now our very lives are at stake. And this we write in pain: that the lives involved are those, alas, of but a fraction of Hungary's Jews . . .

"In the name of our children, our aged, and our defenseless women, in the name of us all as we face certain death, a frightful death, we address this prayer to the Christian community of Hungary . . ."

The answer of Pope Pius XII, already witnessing the collapse of Hitlerism, mind you, and living under the unwelcome but full protection of the Allied armed forces, was: *Silence.*

What lay behind his silence? Eugenio Cardinal Pacelli, from the spring of 1939 Pope Pius XII, former Nuncio in Berlin, always was unduly sympathetic to the German cause. To the worldwide appeal on behalf of the tortured Jewish women and children, he replied that he wished to remain "neutral" in this conflict.

This Pope was never neutral. He repeatedly damned the Russians for alleged "pagan" brutalities and attacked the British and Americans for endangering Rome and bombarding his beloved Monte Cassino, but he steadfastly remained "neutral" in the face of wanton atrocities perpetrated on a million Jewish children, proving the total indifference of this Vicar of Christ toward the suffering of Jews because they were Jews. In front of his very window Jewish families were dragged off to extermination camps, but the Vicar turned the other way. He had just appointed Franz von Papen, who had held the stirrup for Hitler, Councilor of the Holy See.

One cannot serve two masters and Pacelli opted for the one below, not above. Pius XII was certain Hitler would win the war; all his actions were based on this premise. Thus the Vicar of Christ became the chaplain of the Third Reich.

NEO-CATHOLICISM

In January of 1967 Pope Paul VI appointed the German Duke Karl Friedrich zu Lowenstein to the twelve-member International Council of the Church. Radio Vatican made a special announcement of this, the greatest honor the Holy See can bestow upon a layman.

In 1933, the Year of the Wolf in Germany, the Duke took over leadership of the Catholic student society *Unitas,* and from then on during the crucial Hitler decade, served as a fountain of National Socialist pronouncements and affirmations. From this *Unitas* came the utterance, "Catholic thought and the essence of German Fascism are self-identical." He denounced his own cousin for lecturing abroad before a Jewish audience.

The Brown Princeling was a protégé of the pathetic Cardinal Faulhaber who blew first hot then cold as the Swastika rose in the German heavens.

His appointment prompts the question—just how "new" is the "new era" of present-day Catholicism?

NEOFITA, CASA DEI

The House of Catechumens was established in Rome on March 21, 1548, by the Vatican for the specific purpose of compelling conversion of Jews. The house was supported by oppressive taxation of Jews. Popes Pius V and Gregory XIII were especially active in the business of compulsory conversion of Hebrews.

In November, 1604, the chief rabbi of Rome, Joshua Assouth, and his four children were dragged into the house of conversion.

128

For all practical purposes the house was abolished in 1810, at the time of the French occupation. In the Nazi era the chief rabbi of Rome was driven into the hands of the Church by more subtle means.

NEO-NATIONALISM

in Germany can count heavily on the support of the nostalgic clergy. A leader of this group is Josef Cardinal Frings who has become a vociferous apologist for the rise of the brown-shirted heroes of the Hitler decade.

This Archbishop of Cologne blames not the red-handed Germans for the KZ massacres, but rather the Jews themselves. In an extensive interview reported in a West German newspaper, the prelate explained that the Jews of Germany were capitalists who flaunted their immense wealth during the 1920's. The Cardinal also criticized the Jews for their intellectual and cultural influence.

The Cardinal did not even hesitate to question the fact that six million Jews had been most cruelly done to death by his countrymen. He was not sure, he said, that the total was "six million."

For the record it should be stated that Cardinal Frings has always been a man of great compassion. In the early years after Hitler's defeat he helped organize a campaign to prevent "acts of revenge"—Jewish, of course—against "German nationals," even though these "German nationals" were charged before the whole civilized world with the most dastardly crimes against humanity.

NEO-THOMISM

On August 7, 1941, Marshal Pétain sent an inquiry regarding the Vatican's attitude toward the possibility of anti-Jewish measures in Vichy France to the distinguished Catholic leader, Léon Bérard, French Ambassador to the Holy See. The Ambassador replied, after close consultation with the staff of Pius XII, with quotations from Saint

Thomas Aquinas, who, living in the dark ages, held that Jews were destined to be slaves of the Christian rulers, and therefore be barred from all government activity and limited in the professions. The Ambassador also cited the Vatican as not wishing to quarrel with the Vichy Nazi regime over "the Jewish issue."

NEUTRALITY

Would Pope Pius XII have proclaimed neutrality if, instead of a million Jewish children, an equal number of French or Dutch youth had been choked to death by German poison gas? I wonder. I wonder.

NEW TESTAMENT

An anthology of twenty-seven pieces finally constituted in 382 by the Council of Rome as the canon of the Church.

The Synoptics and John were included, but other fragmentary gospels eliminated, such as the Gospel of Peter. Many other "gospels" were circulated in the early centuries, which also purported to be the sayings of Jesus and epistles of evangelists. "The Epistle of Barnabas," "The Shepherd" of Hermas, "The Gospel of the Ebionites" are just a few of the early endeavors of Christian followers to express the prevalent attitudes and beliefs of the early centuries.

The truly verifiable Jesus tradition of the first and second centuries lacks the anti-Semitic interpolations that desecrate the Roman New Testament sponsored by the later Bishops of Rome.

The New Testament is, next to *Mein Kampf,* the most influential anti-Semitic book in print. Both books mention the Jew only in the most derogatory manner: as a traitor, a bloodthirsty murderer, a defiler of temples, a money-changer full of greed, a pitiless enemy of the divine and noble, a scurrilous hater of the divine, a devilish schemer to deprive mankind of salvation.

Both books consider the Jew accursed forever and pitilessly hold *the* Jew responsible for what *a* Jew may or may not have done.

Both books are responsible for the systematic execution not only of millions of men and women but also of children who were guilty of nothing but being born Jews.

Both books have created such hate of the Jew that their readers felt satisfaction in putting even these Jewish children to death in most cruel and torturous ways.

As King Philip II of Spain, defender of Catholicism, ordered: "Do not garrote them before burning; let them feel the full pain of the flames."

Both books have inspired charges against the Jews of conspiring to gain world-wide power over the Christians.

Both books brought Jew hatred to such a pitch that even the dead were not given to relatives to be buried. The persecutors burned the bodies of their Jewish victims as they would foul flesh and dumped their ashes into sewers.

To the Christian churchman the lines above may sound offensive, but the offense is theirs. Ours is only the grief that almost ten million of our kinsmen, among them a million of our little children, were dealt with so bestially.

If the Christians love to drink of the Hebrew wisdom in the New Testament, as it was uttered by the gentle Jew Jeshu and his gentle Jewish Apostles, let them also drink of our tears and our blood, which have flowed freely for two thousand years, because of what the Roman Bishops added to the *Verba Christi* to denigrate the Jew. They have not ceased torturing us.

While *Mein Kampf* is responsible for a greater total of wanton executions than the Catholic churchmen of the New Testament, the Catholic clergy was even more cruel than the Nazis and preceded most burnings with cunning tortures.

Hitler repeatedly pointed out during his successful conference with the representatives of Cardinal Pacelli (later Pope Pius XII) in connection with the Concordat of Collaboration that he was only continuing the fifteen-hundred-year-old "work" of the Catholic Church—namely, to confine and destroy Judaism.

While Nazism may be moribund, anti-Semitic Catholicism is in full bloom. As recently as April, 1966, Bishop Luigi Carli of Segni, who was appointed by the Vatican to head the four-man Ecumenical Curia formulating the "Jewish Declaration," wrote in the clerical review, *Palestro del Clero:* "Judaism carries by its very nature the judgment of condemnation by God."

Mein Kampf is dead, but the New Testament, with its over one hundred anti-Semitic references to the Jews, interpolated by Roman Bishops of the fourth century, lives on to stigmatize, segregate and sting the Jews.

The Jew continues to be depicted as killer and torturer of Christ and greedy defamer of the Temple. In the words of Luigi Carli, the spokesman and head of the Ecumenical Curia, anti-Semitism is not condemned by the Catholic Church, but Judaism is!

NICHOLAS III

This Pope in 1278 made it obligatory for Jews to attend Church sermons in which the Jewish people were described as treacherous God killers. Vincent Ferrer and Raymund of Penaforte, both saints and luminaries of the Catholic Church, also practiced this form of psychological sadism.

Not until 1870 was the monstrous ritual abolished.

NICHOLAS OF CUSA (1401-1464)

This learned Cardinal of Germany traveled in the fifteenth century as a personal delegate of Pope Nicholas V, expressing at all meetings and councils his fanatical hatred of the "God killers." He ordered clerics and civilians alike either to convert Jews or expel them.

NORWICH

In this English town in 1276 a Jew was burned alive for refusing to admit that Jesus was God.

NUMERUS CLAUSUS

or student quota system was practiced in Church schools before it reached the secular institutions. The Jew, ghettoized by the popes and restricted by the bishops, had only rare opportunities for study since education was in large part directed or influenced by clergymen. Here, too, an anti-Semitic measure of the secular modern world finds its early origin in the Church.

O

OATH

On August 12, 1942, the Ministry of Justice of Germany ruled that an oath given by a Jew had no legal validity.

Such a "judicial" attitude was only a resurrection of the medieval Church attitude, which lingered on in the Western world up to the American and French revolutions.

OBERAMMERGAU

This Bavarian town continues, every decade, to stage performances of an anti-Semitic Passion play depicting the suffering of Jesus "at the hands of the perfidious Jews." The play draws an immense tourist crowd that watches the coarse re-enactment of gospel legends in which Judas and the other Jews appear as a fiendish, shaggy, bloodthirsty lot who subject the gentle-looking savior to thorning, beating, spitting, kicking and other abuse.

Christ's Apostles and followers, of course, are played by refined-looking Bavarians whose countenances display German gentility and compassion.

Passion plays derive, in corrupted form, from the "miracle" plays of the Middle Ages. The Oberammergau performance is said to date from a vow undertaken by the community in 1634 to escape the plague. The vicious text of the present Passion Play was written by a local Catholic priest in 1860 and has never failed to arouse peasants as well as city visitors to resentment against the diabolical Jews who were plaguing the Aryan Jesus.

Despite world-wide protests and threats of boycott, the village declared in 1966 that no changes would be made in the text for the performance scheduled in 1970.

OBSCURANTS

Christian writers of catechisms and histories, especially for the young, have managed successfully to veil the totally Jewish milieu of the life of Jesus so that the majority of Christians are not aware of the fact that all—but all—of the people who surrounded and supported Jesus in his lifetime were Hebrews.

These educators in religion describe the mother of Jesus as a "young woman espoused to a man Joseph," who lived "in the country of the Jews." The Apostles are referred to in these school texts as "twelve men chosen by Jesus."

The word "Jew" is used only for an enemy or a bloodthirsty disbeliever.

OLD WINE IN NEW BOTTLES

In the introduction of a revised edition of the New Testament, published in 1959 by "Ars Sacra," the Catholic Professor of Theology Otto Karrer interprets the Jews as a people forever accursed.

In another New Testament "revised" by Father Werner Becker, published in 1962 by Kösel Verlag, the Jews are introduced as "people given to lies and viciousness."

In a 1964 Catholic edition (one million copies) of Holy Scripture, recommended by the Bishop of Rothenburg, Carl

Joseph Leiprecht, the Catholic theologian Peter Ketter writes: "The Jewish people are accursed because they listened to unscrupulous inciters."

All of these "new" editions are still being distributed.

OPPENHEIM

In this German town in the fourteenth century the Jewish population withdrew into their ghetto, set it afire and perished in the flames. The Christians of the town were on the march to kill them for "poisoning" their wells.

In numerous other German towns the Jews were put to death on the same charge. The carnage was horrible in Cologne, Worms, Frankfurt, Erfurt, Colmar—often incited by wandering Catholic "Flagellants."

ORDER OF THE SKULL

The romanticized title of the German *Schutzstaffel*, better known as the SS. The "elite" of the SS, membership in which was rather difficult to attain (therefore alibis of "compulsion" are suspect), were in charge of all concentration camps and their institutional atrocities. It is worth noting that as late as 1946 Archbishop Gröber, later Cardinal Gröber by the grace of "God's Vicar," stated: *"Die SS in Freiburg sind die anständigste* [nicest] *Organization der Partei."*

ORIENTALIZATION

of the Jewish image in Church art and manuscript illumination was of the caricature variety which began in the "Dark Ages" and culminated in the cartoons of *Der Stürmer*.

For example, when the Jew was not portrayed in the horned hat favored by the ecclesiastical law-givers of the Middle Ages, he was usually shown wearing a Saracen turban—although Jews had become "Westernized" in dress during their centuries of domicile in Europe. The artistic repetition of turbans and suchlike exotic props identified Jews, in the minds of the largely illiterate populace, with the Moors, Saracens, Turks, Mongols and other "Asians" who threatened Christian Europe.

OSSERVATORE ROMANO

The official Vatican newspaper that, throughout the Nazi alliance with Mussolini—until the very last day, and beyond —manifested an undaunted spirit of collaboration with the fascist elements, refused to print any news of the horrible atrocities perpetrated upon the hapless Jews and kept even the mass kidnapping in Rome itself of Jewish women and children, destined for execution at Auschwitz, from its readers.

Pope Pius XII, whose grandfather, Marcantonio Pacelli, founded the paper, often read the galley proofs of his chosen news vehicle and would on occasion telephone his criticisms and corrections.

At the height of barbaric brutality by the Gestapo occupation forces in Italy, culminating in the infamous massacre of seventy Jews and hundreds of "other criminals" in the Ardeatine Caves of Rome, Pius XII wrote a personal editorial in *Osservatore Romano* in which he pleaded for *"carita civile"*—"civil compassion"—not by the Nazis, but by the Italian population toward their hard-pressed overlords!

Because of the Pope's admonition, the Italian press refrained for weeks from reporting the latest Nazi *Blutbad* within the confines of the Imperial City. The big news of that day in the press was: "The Pope Enjoys Good Health."

In the evening *Osservatore Romano* repeated again and again the Pope's call for self-control and undiminished succor to the German forces. Not a single word of pity could be spared for the machine-gunned "Jews and other criminals."

The bodies of the slaughtered rotted for months in the

136

foul cave until the stench drove civilians of the neighborhood to give the dead a decent burial.

Monsignor Montini, the present Pope Paul VI, a devoted adviser of the Vicar of Christ, was, like his superior, concerned only with the safety of the Vatican. He complained bitterly to the American representative at the Holy See, Harold H. Tittmann, that the Pope's prestige would suffer were the Allies to bombard Rome.

While the men of the Vatican, and, especially, Pope Pius XII, refused to raise their voices in behalf of the Ardeatine victims, they got religion again when one of the leading anti-Semites of Rome, ex-*Questore* Pietro Caruso, was apprehended for trial after the expulsion of Nazi troops. The Vatican sent no less than a bishop to the trial of the mass-murderer to testify as to Caruso's "good character and fine Catholic background."

It is reminiscent of the German Cardinal Frings' intervention after the war in behalf of elite Nazis. Religion will out: whenever the Jew killings were over, the Christian clergy inveighed against "revengeful Jews."

P

PACEM IN TERRIS

The magnificent spirit of Pope John XXIII in this encyclical moved to strike the accusation of deicide from the pages of Catholic history, but was completely stymied by the "conservative" element of the Vatican commission during the first session of the Ecumenical Council (1961). They could not even muster enough Christian unity to condemn anti-Semitism.

In 1963 a completely watered-down draft of an Ecumenic schema was finally offered under the sponsorship of none less than Pope Paul VI. Archbishop Heenan of Westminster characterized it as totally unrecognizable compared to the text originally shaped in the spirit of John XXIII.

This bastardized schema was fully approved by Pope Paul VI. It omitted Pope John's denial that the Jews were Christ killers; it omitted the point that Christ willed to die and that, if anybody denied him, it was all the people of the world except a small flock of Hebrews. In other words, Jews were the only ones who accepted Christ in his earthly lifetime; no one else did. Therefore the general charge against the Jews as God killers was historically false and theologically biased. Anti-Semitism based on the charge of deicide was to be condemned.

Pope Paul VI, by sponsoring the anti-Semitic schema of the reactionary prelates, placed himself at the head of the inveterate Jew haters in the Church. Equally so, by appointing the blatantly anti-Semitic Bishop Luigi Carli as the head of his Curia to solve the "Jewish Problem," he made a wolf the shepherd.

Just for the record, there is no Jewish problem—the Jews have not persecuted the Catholic churches nor butchered, boiled or beheaded Catholic priests—but there *is* a Catholic problem: Catholic priests and their agents have burned and tortured to death an untold number of Jews.

PAPAL SOLICITUDE

During Charlemagne's reign, Pope Stephen III lodged a sharp complaint with the Bishop of Narbonne "that Jewish people on French soil enjoy full equality with Christians and that Christian men and women defile their souls by living under the same roof with the traitors of Christ."

Under Louis the Pious, Charlemagne's successor, the Bishop of Lyon addressed a note to the prelate of Narbonne, expressing great concern "because I see the virgin bride of Christ [Gentile girls] sit down to eat in the company of whores [Jewish girls]."

Almost the identical words were used by the Brown Shirts to condemn Judaeo-Christian fraternizing.

Pope Benedict XIV (*A Quo Primum,* 1751) warned against any intimacy with the Hebrews, referring obviously to Pope Innocent II (1198-1216), who wrote in an encyclical: "Jews are like a rat in the sack or a snake in the bosom. Christians therefore may not enter the service of Jews; no public position may be bestowed upon Jews; no Christian may seek the cure of a Jewish physician."

All this and more Brown Shirt Vaticanism may be found in the *Bullarum Romanum* under the headings of the Popes Nicholas IV, Paul IV, Pius V, Gregory XIII, Clement VIII.

Indeed, there is not a single Pope on record who was not anti-Semitic in deed, word, or implication except good Pope John XXIII.

PARIS

Upon the orders of Pope Gregory IX (1242) to destroy all Hebrew literature, twenty-four cartloads of Hebrew sacred books were burned in Paris.

PASSAU

In this Bavarian town in 1478 a local priest charged Jews with breaking a holy wafer (host). The accused were tortured and burned. The synagogue was "converted" into a church, which still publicizes the "desecration"—of the host, of course.

PASSION PLAYS

because of their Christological character invariably depicted the Jewish characters as killers or traitors (e.g., Judas). Those still to be seen today, of which the most famous is performed at the Bavarian town of Oberammergau, are no different in their insistent denigration of the Jews.

For example, a Passion play which has been presented for more than fifty years in a Catholic church in Union City, New Jersey, was recently analyzed by the American Jewish Congress in these terms:

"In the play, Judas is presented as a caricature identical with Julius Streicher's stereotype of a Jew in *Der Stürmer*. . . .

"The Jewish priests are depicted as brutish louts, cunning and corrupt. . . .

"The climax is the Crucifixion, accompanied by an electrical storm whose terrible lightning and rolling thunder constitute a magnificent spectacle—and which reduced many of the children in the audience to hysteria. . . .

"The entire production is a searing, hate-filled indictment of Jewry. The Jews are satanic; the Christians are divine disciples of the Lord Jesus."

Thus Union City's Passion play lives up to its advance billing as "America's Oberammergau"—indeed, it goes Oberammergau one better: the Bavarian Passion play is only staged every ten years, while Union City's extravaganza of Jew-hate is given weekly performances every year during the Lenten season!

PASTORAL ANTI-SEMITISM

"Degenerate Judaism together with Freemasonry is the carrier of mammoth capitalism. To fight the evil influence of Judaism is not only the privilege but the duty of every good Christian. . . . A dam should be erected against spiritual dirt and immorality which threatens the world from the Jews."—Gföllner, Bishop of Linz (Austria) : Pastoral Letter of January 21, 1933.

PASTORELLI

A shepherds' Crusade in 1320 led by a berserk parish priest and a fanatical Benedictine monk. It began and ended with the massacre of French Jews, and was widely favored by the Church.

On the road to Carcassonne five hundred Jews took refuge from the Pastorelli in a fortification where, after their food gave out, they killed their children and women, themselves perishing sword in hand.

The siege near Carcassonne, six centuries before the bombardment of the Warsaw ghetto, reminds us that the history of Jewish resistance to Christian savagery has been perforce a long one.

PAUL IV (1555-1559)

This Pope instigated the burning alive of sixty convert Jews for "pretense." He enforced the ghetto rules in Rome and the wearing of the yellow leper badge; excluded Jews from all professions and trades except manual work; destroyed all but one synagogue in his domain; banned all contact of Jews with Christians, as well as the reading of the Talmud.

He appointed the sadistic Cesare Galúaba "commissioner of faith" for the Italian town of Ancona. Galúaba terrorized sixty-three Jews into conversion. Twenty-three other men and women, whose names are handed down to us in contemporary chronicles, refused baptism; they were all hanged and then burned on the Piazza della Mostra.

Only some Turkish Jews escaped the holocaust. Sultain Suleiman II obtained their release by threatening the Pope with retribution.

Not until French occupation of Ancona did the Jews obtain security in the city. Even then, in 1797, a fanatical clergy incited the populace to sack the ghetto. In 1826 Pope Leo XII re-established in Ancona the ghetto that had been eliminated by Napoleon Bonaparte.

Finally the Revolution of 1848 brought full freedom from Catholic persecution to the Jews of Ancona.

PERDITIO

"Disaster" is the name Pope Gregory I (590-604), the father of the "Historic Church," assigned to Judaism, a

141

faith he stigmatized as shot through with perfidy. This great Pope spewed out a colorful stream of gutter-abuse against the Jews. He cursed them as "wild asses" and "dragons of poison" with "their hearts a den of beasts."

PERFIDY

of the Jews was included in the Catholic Good Friday liturgy: *"Oremus et pro perfidis Judaeis."* This has been omitted recently. Christian liturgy abounds in negative references to the Jews.

PERU

In 1639 twelve Portuguese Jews were burned at the stake by the Inquisition.

PETER OF BLOIS

Archdeacon at the English town of Bath in the twelfth century, who wrote *Against the Perfidious Jews*. He took the title for his tract from a Good Friday prayer of the Catholic liturgy. His conclusions: "The Jews are beasts. You can see it on their faces."

The gentle deacon was often quoted by Sir Oswald Mosley, British sympathizer with the Nazi movement.

PETER OF CLUNY

One of the highly revered figures in Catholic history, who, during the Second Crusade, implored King Louis VII of France to punish the Jews since they were worse than the Saracens. They defiled Christ and robbed the Christians. They should be forced to pay for the Crusade, yet they should not be killed immediately—rather, they should be made to live under constant torture.

We have here a striking similarity with Hitler's depriving all European Jews of their funds to help finance his wars, and then letting them suffer a painful degradation and captivity before extermination.

PETER THE HERMIT (b. 1050)

A French monk of Amiens with a venomous tongue, who was the most ferocious anti-Semitic Crusader of the Catholic clergy.

PETER THE VENERABLE

Abbot of Cluny, who admonished the Crusaders: "What does it profit to persecute enemies of Christianity outside when evil Jews in our midst deface Christ with impunity?"

An almost identical appeal was made by Reinhard Heydrich to the Germans not to wait for attacks on France and England, but to destroy first the Jew, the enemy within their borders.

PHILIP III (1245-1285)

upon repeated urging of the clergy required the Jews of France to attach a horn-shaped figure to their badge. Even Michelangelo accepted the Vatican suggestion that he crown his "Moses" with Devil's horns.

PIUS V

in 1569 expelled the Jews from the Papal States except for Rome (the Bull *Hebraeorum gens*).

PIUS VI

As late as 1775 this pope issued an edict compelling the Jews in the Papal States to listen, after their Sabbath services, to anti-Semitic "conversion" harangues delivered in the synagogues by unscrupulous clerics.

It was only a year before America's Declaration of

Independence, yet the Pope's bull reiterated the most severe restrictions upon Jewish life, from ghettoism to the yellow badge of the Middle Ages.

With the rising spirit of revolution in America and France, freedom riots occurred in Rome in 1793. The Vatican blamed these riots on the Jews as enemies of the old order, and a vicious pogrom followed in the Roman ghetto.

In 1798 French Revolutionary armies occupied Rome, and for the first time in over fifteen hundred years the Jews of Rome could breathe freely.

PIUS VII

This pope demanded in 1815 that all Jews, who had been given civil rights under the French occupation, be removed from all public offices in the Papal State.

His successor, Pope Leo XII, asked that the Jews be punished since "they had tortured and murdered Jesus."

Incidentally, this last quotation was repeated verbatim in public during "Holy Week" of 1965 by Pope Paul VI, the Ecumenist.

PIUS IX

As late as 1870 this Pope rejected a petition of Jewish inhabitants of Rome to abolish the ghetto. A year later King Victor Emmanuel, disregarding the Pope, had the gates removed.

PIUS XII

See Nazi Vaticanism; *Osservatore Romano; Stellvertreter.*

POBIEDONOSTZEV, KONSTANTIN PETROVICH

Procurator of the Russian Orthodox "Holy Synod," who proposed an *"Endlösung"* of the Jewish problem in the latter nineteenth century: the expulsion of one-third of the Jews, forcible conversion of the "better" third, and starvation by internment of the last third. After the assassination by radicals of Czar Alexander II (1881) the slogan of the Russian Orthodoxy was: Kill the Jews who killed Jesus and the Czar. Great pogroms, inspired by the clergy, swept Russia. They began with Easter Sunday church assemblies and Jews in 160 towns were attacked, mutilated and killed. Only through the intervention of foreign governments, especially the United States of America, were the hapless victims permitted to leave Russian territory.

POGROM

Russian word meaning "devastation," an apt name, indeed, for the officially directed attacks against the Jewish communities of Russia. Pogroms in Russia were too numerous even to list. In a single week during October, 1905, 670 pogroms took place, encouraged if not invoked by the Orthodox clergy, leaving thousands of Jewish men, women and children dead or mutilated.

The United States, as it had after previous pogroms, prevailed upon the Czarist government to permit emigration of the Jews to its shores. Czar Nicholas II protested loudly to intercessors from abroad: "But they are Christ killers!"

POLAND

Major anti-Semitic activity began with the Council of Breslau (now Wroclaw) in 1267, which advocated the Jew badge and the ghetto. With the rise to power of the

Catholic Church under the Jagiello dynasty, the lot of the Jews became unbearable.

The Catholic Church charged ritual murder and desecration of holy wafers to arouse the populace. In 1399 thirteen Jews were burned alive in Posen for "breaking the host."

Incited by clergy of the Eastern Orthodox Church, hordes of Cossacks under their hetman, Bogdan Chmielnicki, fell upon Poland (1648-1658), massacring over one hundred thousand Jews in the most cruel manner to protect Christianity from "the Jewish devils." Victims were mutilated by Ukrainians and Tartars alike. Infants were slit alive, women were ripped open and then sewn together with live rats in their bowels.

In 1664 Catholic seminary students attacked the Jews in Lemberg after a ritual murder charge.

Attacks and pogroms continued well into the twentieth century. During the German siege of the Warsaw Ghetto in the Second World War, Poles rendered no aid to the Jews; there are on record numerous cases of denunciation of Jews in hiding to the Gestapo in Warsaw.

In 1946, a year after the war, inhabitants of the town of Kielce massacred half of their Jewish population— over forty—who had escaped the German concentration camps. The Polish archbishop saw this as a proper occasion to make vicious remarks about the Christ killers.

POLISH CATHOLICS

Hitler declared: "I as a German Catholic ask only what is permitted to Polish Catholics. To be anti-Semitic is not to be anti-Catholic."

"In Rome, under the dominion of the Church, the Jews occupied a position that we should be satisfied to see restored. The Church used every weapon against the Jews, even the Inquisition. Christ Himself was a pioneer in the fight against Judaism."

Thus spake Hitler.

And soon after these words he adopted the Catholic

Church's *"Endlösung"* of the Jewish problem: extermination of the Hebrews themselves, men, women and children.

POLISH CHARTER

of protection was granted to the Jews in 1264 by Boleslaw the Pious, King of Poland. Jews were given, as *servi camerae* or "servants of the Court," a guarantee of personal freedom and professional security. Religious as well as physical inviolability was assured.

In 1267 the Church Council at Breslau protested these "outrageous" privileges with which the Jews had been endowed by the gentry of Poland. The Council demanded segregation of Jews into ghettos, the wearing of leper badges, and discrimination against Jews in trade.

King Casimir the Great (1333-1370) strengthened the Charter but the Catholic Church did not cease its relentless anti-Semitism. Charges of ritual murder, well poisoning and host desecration were raised again and again.

In the fifteenth century the Papal Inquisitory Delegate, St. John Capistrano, roused the low clergy of Poland to a high pitch of anti-Semitic frenzy. Jews in Cracow and Lwow were massacred. Small Unitarian groups that appealed in the sixteenth and seventeenth centuries for religious tolerance were soon suppressed by the Catholic hierarchy.

The Jesuits in Poland were particularly aggressive in their anti-Jewish hostility which has persisted until this very day.

POLNA

In this Bohemian town in 1900 local Jews were accused by the clergy of drinking the blood of Christian children. Professor Thomas Masaryk, later President of Czechoslovakia, defended them.

was, if such a monstrosity is conceivable, more cruel than the Spanish. The unfortunate Jews, and Marranos who had been indicted for "Judaizing" (relapsing), languished in filthy dungeons, chained by both hands with their backs to the wall, beaten and otherwise molested by fanatical guards. To narrate the rest would not be helpful since no pen can amply describe the bestiality of the Catholic persecutors.

The Inquisition slogan *Justitia et Misericordia* is characteristic of Christian Jew-hatred: the words of angels, on the fiery tongue of the Devil. Some Popes—for example, Nicolas V, Clement VI and Innocent VI—exhorted inquisitors to be especially severe.

POSEN

The Archbishop of this Polish city, after the death of the benevolent King Casimir the Great (1333-1370), charged the local rabbi and thirteen elders of the temple with having "bloodied" three consecrated wafers belonging to the Dominican Church.

All the accused were burned over a slow fire. The property of all was "sequestered" by the Dominican Order.

POTOCKI, VALENTIN

A Polish count who became a convert to Judaism. He was apprehended at the behest of the Catholic clergy, condemned by the ecclesiastical court, and burned at the stake in the city of Vilna in front of the cathedral (May, 1749).

PRAGUE

In 1389 a Catholic priest in Prague accused Jewish children at play of having thrown sand on his sacred host.

When he incited the mob to a riot, over three thousand Jews became its victims and the synagogue was burned. Some of the unfortunate were tied to the stake by their feet, "so as to quicker reach their Devil's abode."

Prague was one of the many cities along the route of the crusading protectors of the Grail to have its Jewish citizens put to the cross or the sword.

PRANAITIS, JUSTIN

A Catholic priest, who published in 1893 a pamphlet entitled *The Christian in the Jewish Talmud* in the Russian capital of St. Petersburg, "proving" among other things that the Jews were using the blood of Christian children in the baking of matzoth.

He became in 1911 the "expert" witness for the prosecution at the notorious Beiliss trial. His colleague in defamation was Archimandrite Ambrosius of the Russian Orthodox Church.

PRIVILEGIA ODIOSA

Restrictive legislation reducing the civil status of Jews —for instance, in the Christian Codex Theodosianus, the prohibition of "mixed marriages" under penalty of death and disbarment from all official positions in the government, military, judiciary. (Cf. The National Socialist regime in Hitler's Germany.) Thus the canonical as well as imperial laws of Christian Rome and Constantinople were basically anti-Semitic.

PROPAGANDA

of an anti-Semitic nature up to the nineteenth century was primarily in the hands of clerics. They did the preaching, writing, and producing of plays and festivals. There was no way of reaching the masses except through the

Church, and the Church was vividly anti-Semitic. Even where schools were not entirely in the hands of the clergy, the latter had sole jurisdiction over classes in religion.

Against this massive one-way tirade hardly a voice could be raised even by well-wishers for reason, tolerance and justice; not until the American and French revolutions had broken the back of despotically entrenched churchism, and separated Church from State.

PROTECTORS OF JEWS

Throughout World War II Italy's armed forces successfully resisted all German efforts to apprehend and deport Jews, Italian or alien. They did not permit the arrest of Jews in territories under their protection, African or European. On many occasions they freed Jewish internees from the hand of the French Vichy police.

The Rumanian general, Antonescu, was able to protect most of the Jewish citizens in Old Rumania, as General Mannerheim saved the Jews of Finland, and King Christian X those of Denmark.

However, Pope Pius XII was determined in his infinite Christian charity to remain "neutral" in the war of ten million Nazi killers against a million Jewish infants and children.

Incidentally, all the generals and the noble Danish king remained unmolested, except for a few letters of protest from Berlin. But Pope Pius XII prayed often and publicly for the victory of the forces of liberation from atheism and socialism.

PROTOCOLS OF THE LEARNED ELDERS OF ZION

One of the many anti-Semitic pamphlets prepared and distributed by the Czarist government after Russia's defeat at the hands of the Japanese (1905). The Jew was to be the scapegoat for a corrupt and discredited government.

Similar pamphlets for a similar purpose were concocted by the National Socialists after Germany's defeat by the Allies. The Jews had caused the defeat. The Jews are at the bottom of any and all Christian misfortune.

In 1921 a correspondent of the London *Times* uncovered the plagiarism of half the *Protocols* from a satire on Napoleon III written by Maurice Joly, a French attorney. Other portions were plagiarized from a story by Hermann Goedsche and other fictional sources.

The forgery of the *Protocols* gives a clear insight into the sickeningly dishonest mentality of anti-Semites.

PROUDHON, PIERRE-JOSEPH (1809-1865)

A French typesetter with little education but a flair for socialist bravado, who found the Jews an easy target for popular libel: "The Jews are stupid and politically inept. Otherwise they would have accepted Jesus as God instead of opposing him. With their messianic stubbornness they placed themselves outside the pale of mankind."

Everything else Proudhon said about the Jews stems from the altar-born hate of his childhood, which he never overcame. And this in spite of his turning in later years against the Church! With him it is the same as with all the other socialist anti-Semites, from Marx to Stalin: they turned away from the Church, even against it, but they remained steadfast in Jew hate.

PRYNNE, WILLIAM (1600-1669)

A Puritan divine who called upon Heaven and Hell to stop Oliver Cromwell's decision to readmit Jews to England (1659). He quoted other objecting voices as saying, "We must now all turn Jews."

This fanatical pamphleteer actually prevented, single-handed, the official return of the Jews; Cromwell's government admitted them only unofficially. Prynne's pamphlet,

A Short Demurrer to the Jews' Long Discontinued Remitter into England, was distributed in church and school throughout the island.

RADULPH

A French monk of the Second Crusade who wandered about Europe preaching violence against the killers of Christ. Without exception the doors of the churches were opened to his homily of hate. The mobs attacked the Jews with the cry, "Hep! Hep!—an easy abbreviation for the illiterate of *Hiersolyma est perdita*—"Jerusalem is lost").

RAMERU

In this French town at the time of the Second Crusade (1147-1149) Rabbi Jacob Tam was stabbed five times in the head by a clergy-led mob as punishment for the "five injuries inflicted" upon Jesus. Church-instigated pogroms also occurred in the German towns of Würzburg, Speyer, and so on.

RATISBON

A town in Germany where in the crusading era all Jews were led to the Danube. Those who refused baptism were drowned in the blue waters.

RECESWINTH (649-672)

This Spanish king appeared in person before the Eighth Council of Toledo (653) to denounce the Jews as wormy Christ killers. With the full consent of the assembled clergy he stripped the Jews of all civil rights. He imposed, among other things, relentless floggings and hair extraction for any sign of "anti-Christian" behavior. All Jews had to sign an order of obedience that prohibited the observance of their religious rituals. Violators were to be burned alive.

RELIGIO LICITA

Judaism was protected under pagan Rome as *religio licita,* a lawful or permitted religion. Pagan Rome treated the Jews no differently than its other subject nations, respecting in general their distinctive religious observances. Emperor worship was rarely enforced in synagogues throughout the Empire. Jews had been traveling, working, settling and trading in Roman lands for many centuries before Jesus. Dispersion was voluntary and wide.

With the rise of dominant Christianity, Judaism became illicit; the only question remaining was how severely it would be oppressed by the Christian authorities.

After fifteen centuries this judgment still stands: "Present-day Judaism is illegal before God and as a religion carries by its very nature the judgment of condemnation by God."

These are the exact words written by Bishop Luigi Carli, whom Pope Paul VI chose, of all prelates, to head the Curia committee charged by Vatican II with preparation of the official "Declaration on the Jewish problem."

Carli's insolent and vicious attack on the Jews appeared near the close of the Ecumenical Council in the Vatican review, *Palestro del Clero.*

Pope Paul VI has not only endorsed Carli's promulgation, but sponsored it and thereby identified himself with traditional Vatican anti-Semitism. Paul VI, unlike the late Pope John XXIII, whose nobility transcended the Dark Ages, embodies the Catholic motto: *"Semper idem*—Always the same."

RELIGIOUS LIBERTY

"Unfettered liberty of religious thought and freedom of speech are the worst plagues of all." So declared Pope Gregory XVI (d. 1846) in the encyclical *Mirari Vos*.

Another Vatican luminary, Pope Leo XII, wrote in 1885: "The equal toleration of all religions is nothing but atheism."

RENAN, ERNEST (1823-1892)

French historian, originally trained for the Catholic priesthood, who can be regarded as the father of anti-Semitic anthropology. He considered the Jew a cunning Semite who endeavors to master "the honest Aryan." The Jew is cancer eating into the flesh of Christian Aryans. The Jew does not work, he only exploits. The Jew is selfish and cowardly, while the Aryan is given to self-sacrifice.

Alfred Rosenberg, Hitler's personal anthropologist, called Renan "the man who discovered the soul of the German."

RESPECT

Some have said I should be more respectful writing about the Christian Bishops since they were men of God.

Perhaps they were.

How shall I speak of the men who preach that my little grandchildren are the poisonous seed of the Devil?

How shall I speak of the men who call my faith accursed by God?

How shall I speak of the men who refuse to condemn the vile hate against my nation, indeed teach it?

How shall I speak of the men who have a history of ripping open the throats of my ancestors like leopards?

They are men of books, you say. But in their books, old and new, from the beginning of time as they count it, my people are depicted with the horns of Satan, with the fangs of Beelzebub, with the greed of Lucifer and the lust of Lilith. All that is evil in their minds they attribute to us, until we appear to the whole Christian world as an apparition from hell.

I shall speak of the Christian Bishops as men of God when they throw off the old clothes of malice and cleanse their Gospels and catechisms and prayers of the infamies with which they have besmirched us. If they do that, there will be a great rejoicing on earth and in heaven.

In spite of the presumption of two thousand clerics and clerks in Rome, the Chosen People are my people. We are still here after two thousand years of the bishops' exhortation, "Burn the Jews!" We feel chosen to stand for the word of God, which they have made a heavy task indeed, an almost unbearably costly privilege.

The Roman Bishops think that they have lifted from our shoulders the mantle of being God's own people and appropriated it for themselves. This is no better than Hitler's claiming that Christ was a Teuton. No one can steer the hand of God—perhaps they indeed think that God is dead and that His Vicar has taken over.

RIBEAUVILLE

In this French town were lodged a score of Jews who in 1331 had been turned over by Louis of Bavaria to the Sieur de Ribeaupierre as surety for a loan of 400 marks in silver. All the Jews were garroted for being poisoners of wells.

RIGORD, PHILIP AUGUSTUS

This monk of twelfth-century France was one of the many medieval clerics who gave "eyewitness" accounts of Jewish murders of Christians. He reports in his *Gesta Philippi Augusti:* "The Jews who dwelt in Paris were wont

155

every year on Easter Day to go down secretly into underground vaults and kill a Christian as a sacrifice in contempt of the Christian faith."

RINDFLEISCH

A devout German nobleman who in 1298 spread word through the town of Rottingen that Jews had spit out a blessed wafer (host) that a group of churchgoers tried to force upon them. Herr Rindfleisch and the infuriated mob set upon the Jewish families of the town and dragged them to the stake. All were burned alive.

This Church-supported *Judenschächter* took his followers through Germany and Austria, murdering the Jewish population. Over one hundred thousand became victims of their wanton atrocities.

The role of individual priests in the ravaged towns during the pogroms is sickening to report.

RITUAL MURDER

This libel, which stamps the Jew a vampire, has been so attractive to Christian anti-Semites that even modern theologians have often hesitated to denounce it. Churches in Austria, for instance, still carry "memorial" tablets depicting the Jew as a ritual killer.

In all cases of ritual murder during Holy Week, the Christian clergy was the accuser. In 1171 in Blois, France, forty Jews were tortured and burned for crucifying and bleeding a child. As late as the eighteenth century Pope Benedict XIV issued a bull blessing an alleged ritual victim, Andrew of Rinn (1755). In this bull the Pope expressed his strong conviction that Jews would murder Christian children because of their "hate of Jesus."

The Catholic Church has not only acquiesced in the veneration of "victims of Jewish calumny" but sponsored the apotheosis of the little corpses through beatification, canonization and sanctification. See also *Vampires*.

156

ROHLING, AUGUST (Father)

Professor of Catholic theology at the University of Vienna, author of *The Talmud Jew* (1871), a scurrilous "Hep! Hep!" attack on the Jewish people. With Wilhelm Marr—another precursor of Josef Goebbels—the coiner of the term "anti-Semite."

ROME

The first expulsion of Jews from Rome was directed by Pope John XXII, but curtailed by King Robert of Sicily (1321).

The second expulsion occurred in 1944 by order of the Gestapo and with the silent consent of Pope Pius XII.

ROUEN

In this French town the Crusaders of the eleventh century fell upon the Jews and murdered all who refused baptism.

RUMANIA

The Orthodox Church here made numerous ritual murder charges against the Jews as late as the nineteenth century. Medieval anti-Semitic measures forced upon a weak government by the clergy brought about foreign intervention. The Berlin Congress of 1878 ordered the Rumanian government to grant the Jews civil rights. Failure of Rumania to comply brought about large Jewish emigration, mainly to the United States.

The Rumanian clergy gave strong support to the World War II alliance with the German Nazi government.

SALE OF JEWS

was widely practiced by secular as well as ecclesiastic authorities in Catholic Europe up to the eighteenth century, when the French revolution breached the traditional status of the Jew as a serf or *"Kammerknecht"* of the king or bishop.

In the doctrine of Saint (*sic!*) Augustinus and Saint (*sic!*) Thomas Aquinas, the Jew must forever be a slave of the ruling Lord; in the doctrine of Martin Luther, the Jew has to be reduced to the status of a slave of the serfs, otherwise his deviltry might contaminate *"den deutschen Bürger."*

Catholic rulers used to demand ransom from Jewish communities for the privilege of leaving their domain alive. The alternative, of course, was certain death on the pyre. Jewish communities in neighboring and even faraway lands had to raise funds to buy off the Christian rulers of their brethren.

The cynical and barbaric maneuver by which Hitler's agent, Eichmann, endeavored to sell one million Jews for the equivalent of ten thousand trucks was only a modern version of the extortion widely practiced in the past by Catholic regents.

SALVATION

An academic survey of Catholics and Protestants in Germany indicates that 86 percent of those questioned hold that members of the Hebrew faith are beyond the bounds of salvation.

We Jews desire no other salvation but from the Christians. The Devil himself could do no worse to us than have the churches.

SCHIRACH, BALDUR VON (b. 1907)

Convicted Nazi war criminal who was entrusted by the Catholic Church in the Pacelli Concordat of Collaboration with the mobilization of Germany's Catholic youth groups. The Lutheran bishops' conference had already given its consent to Protestant youth being enlisted in official units, which, like all Nazi organizations, were shock-troops in the war against the Jews.

SCHOENERER, GEORG VON

Professional anti-Semite of that unsavory variety that has neither conviction nor faith, but takes advantage of an existing trend and makes the most outrageous statements to place itself "on the crest of the wave." In the late nineteenth century Schönerer rode the ground-swell of Jew hate maintained by Austrian and German clergy.

Wherever the anti-Semitic "surf's up," Schönerers will be found.

SEGREGATION

In a decree of 1442 Pope Eugenius IV proclaimed: "We order that henceforth Christians may not eat or drink with Jews, not bathe or cohabit with them. They may not hold public office nor receive civic honors."

The zealous Pontiff never saw his decree take full effect in Europe. Hitler did.

SEMI-JUDAEUS

Derogatory reference to Christians of Semitic birth commonly applied by zealous Catholic protagonists during the Middle Ages and the Renaissance. The comparable term of *Halb-Juden* was adopted by the Nazi "blood purists."

SERFS

During the Middle Ages many rulers of Europe adopted the social reforms proposed by the Catholic Church Fathers and reduced the Jews in their domains to *servi camerae* (servants of the court). As recommended by the saintly Thomas Aquinas, illustrious philosopher of Catholicism, Jews were treated as cattle. They were bought and sold in deals between nobles and kings. On this issue Luther did not differ from the Vatican: the Jew was rightless, a means of exchange.

Pope Innocent III (1198-1216) declared that the Jews are to live in "perpetual servitude." The Third Lateran Council (1179) emphasized that the Jews were "subjects" of the Christians.

SEVILLE

Fernando Martinez, archdeacon of this town in 1391 mobilized the populace in a pogrom against the Jewish quarter. Four thousand Jews were killed; the rest were forcibly enrolled in the religion of love.

From Seville the Church-inspired pogroms spread to Spanish towns everywhere—except, of course, in Moorish territory. Synagogues were converted, together with pitifully few Jewish survivors, to the "True Faith." In some ghettos not a single Jew survived, and the local Christians had their new "House of God" to themselves.

SHYLOCK

The well-known dramatic figure of a vengeful, merciless Jew, brimful of hate for Christians, appears like the materialization of a chimera from the mind of one of the anti-Semitic Fathers of the early Church. Shakespeare, who never saw any Jews in his lifetime, since all Jews had been deported from England in 1290, created this *dramatis persona* from a story by Gregorio Leti, biographer of Pope Sixtus V, which was published in Venice in 1587. There is only one difference: The flesh-greedy merchant in Leti's story is Paul Secchi, a Christian, who wagers a pound of flesh from the body of the Jew (Sampson Ceneda) against the Jew's thousand crowns. The Pope intervenes and both pay a fine.

Shakespeare, employing an old trick of the writer's trade, merely switched roles and made the Jew the villain, which gave him a wide-open opportunity to paint vividly a monstrous Hebrew with all the failings and devilishness the populace loved to hate.

The Church of England, by appropriate sermon, prayer and catechism, kept fresh the image of the treacherous Jew. It was this monstrous image which Shakespeare tried to imitate at the expense of twisting an old Venetian story.

SIEGBURG

In this little German town in 1287 all Jewish inhabitants were accused of killing a Christian boy, Johänneken, and draining his blood. All the Jews were burned. Later the Church sanctified the child.

This sort of deliberate beatification or canonization of little corpses lent credibility to the preposterous tales of blood-drinking Hebrews, which even then were rejected as stupid superstition by enlightened men.

SION, SISTERS OF

Catholic religious order founded in 1844 to accomplish the conversion of the children of Jews to Christianity. One means adopted by the order was the establishing of schools where Jewish (and Moslem) pupils were welcome, as well as Christian children. Conversion was disowned as a goal during the 1930's in favor of a policy of fostering understanding and recognition of Judaism among Catholics, and of succor to Jews during World War II. In 1967 the Sisters of Sion began publication of a journal, *Sidic,* which aims to record, criticize and advance progress toward Catholic acceptance of Jews and Judaism. A little candle in the still-darkened world of age-old condemnation by the Christian Churches!

SISEBUT (612-621)

This Spanish King, who preceded Ferdinand and Isabella by almost nine hundred years, demanded that Jews convert or leave the country. The Church used every means, such as the secret conversion of children, to force the cross upon the harassed Jewish people.

SOCIAL JUSTICE

An anti-Semitic publication sponsored during the 1930's by Father Charles E. Coughlin of the Shrine of the Little Flower in Michigan. This radio priest was Hitler's most effective public relations man in the United States through his virulent, libelous attacks upon the "international Jewish banker."

The magazine reached a circulation of one million before it was banned from the mails during World War II. Much of the material published by the cunning priest was reprinted from Nazi news services. The good Father also ran serially the fraudulent, plagiarized *Protocols of Zion.*

SPINOZA, BARUCH (1632-1677)

Brilliant Jewish philosopher living in Holland among Portuguese Marranos. For his humanistic attitude he was attacked by both Protestants and Catholics alike. His books were on the Index of the Vatican and were burned by Protestants.

To avoid disaster for their whole community, after repeated warnings and admonitions to cease, the elders and the rabbis of the great Amsterdam synagogue expelled Spinoza from their house of worship. Spinoza continued to live in Amsterdam, in later years in Rijnsberg and The Hague, but no longer could the hard-pressed Jews be held responsible for the anticlericalism found in his noble writings.

On his grave, a year after his burial in The Hague, the Dutch Protestant minister, Rev. Carolus Tuinman, had a stone placed, engraved: "Here lies B.D.S. Spit on his grave. Would that his word were buried with him. His pestilence would not devour any more! Renegade Jew!"

STAMFORD

In this English town in the thirteenth century a ghoulish peasant, out plundering Jewish victims, was killed by another marauder. He was immediately canonized by request of the Bishop of Lincoln. This brought a great influx of pilgrims to the town, since the corpse of the bandit performed healing miracles. The desire to create a pilgrim attraction was a major factor in Christian ritual trials.

STANGL, PAUL

SS—Hauptsturmführer and Commander of Nazi extermination camps Solibar and Treblinka. With the help of Austrian clergy escaped his just prosecutors in 1948 into Italy, where the Catholic Bishop Hudal, by Stangl's own assertion, supplied false paper to Brazil.

Stangl was only one of many of the Hitler elite whose flight from justice was made possible by an anti-Semitic clergy.

STATUTES OF VALLADOLID

warned Spanish Christians against food-poisoning by Jewish merchants (1412).

STELLVERTRETER

This German translation of "the Vicar" has become a personal cognomen for Pius XII, the Pope who refused to lend his high office and supreme moral authority over all Roman Catholics in defense of the one million children and five million adults being scientifically exterminated in German ghetto camps. He was the first to know of the immensity of the crime since more than one third of the German officers, Gestapo and SS men involved in the apprehending, transportation and gassing were, like Hitler himself, of the Catholic faith.

When Catholic clergymen, officers and high-ranking civilians in the east of Europe reported the gruesome details of German anti-Semitic atrocities, such as choking Jewish women and children to death in sealed cattle cars, Pope Pius XII refused to see the bearers of such news and brushed aside pleas from Italian friends of the Vatican and some of his conscience-stricken cardinals and bishops.

He, the Vicar of Christ, would not even allow Church periodicals to report the deeds of the Nazis in their ghetto camps. (He did, however, throughout the same period permit the publication of vile anti-Semitic essays on "Jewish decadence" by Catholic Nazi writers.)

He would not ask German Catholics to refrain from bayoneting or gassing Jewish women and children because —mark the Vicar's pastoral tact!—any such admonition "could create in the German Catholic soldier pangs of conscience that might interfere with the war effort."

He would not make an appeal to Chancellor Hitler for pity because "that might worsen the position of the Jews." (How the position of a Jewish woman or child being asphyxiated in a gas chamber could be worsened is beyond any man's imagination.)

Finally, any public or private remonstrances expressed to the German Ambassador in Rome would mean a breach of Vatican neutrality in the war!

This Pope, on repeated occasions breached Vatican

neutrality, but always in protest against the Allies, never against Hitler.

The Pope did intervene directly through his German bishops, and successfully so, to save the lives of thousands of mentally and physically disabled Catholics who had been doomed to a "mercy death" by Nazi decree. He was also instrumental in saving the lives of thousands of Catholics of Jewish origin, converts who were already in the hands of the Gestapo.

But he would not cry out in behalf of a Jewish Jew, even if such persons were taken in front of his very eyes, from the Jewish ghetto in Rome. The majority of Jewish victims taken by the Germans in Rome were women and children. The men joined the partisans in the hills; the old and the women remained with their children, certain that the saintly men of the Vatican, at whose very steps they cowered, would prevent the garroting of the helpless.

Monstrous conquerors of history, hot with the fury of war, have disdained murdering women and children. But the Germans did not. And the hand of the Pope was raised, not to stop the butchery of the innocent, but to bless the German Ambassador, Weizsäcker, who was leaving the Holy See to report gleefully to Herr Ribbentrop: "Although under pressure from all sides, the Pope has not let himself be drawn into any censure of the deportation of Jews from Rome."

Such is the tragic role played by the Vicar of Christ. Yet let not Protestants turn away, satisfied that history chose the guilty one outside their ranks. The Protestant bishops bore no lighter a mark of Cain than the Vatican. They were no less prompt to ring their churchbells when the last Jew in their see was dragged away to oblivion. They, too, glorified Hitlerism at its festivals and victory celebrations.

Look at the photographs of their participation and note the cheerful expressions on their faces! They enjoyed the Hitler happenings and still keep their memory fresh. Faces don't lie, and the faces of Protestant as well as

Catholic clergymen of the Brown Decade display not the benign smile of the gentle Jew Jesus but the arrogant grin of Lucifer.

STOECKER, ADOLF (b. 1835)

Demagogical court preacher of Kaiser Wilhelm I at Berlin, member of the Prussian Diet, and professed "Christian Socialist." He successfully used Lutheran as well as Catholic teachings to direct the German workingman's resentment of the rising power of industry and capitalism against the Jew.

The bankers and industrial Junkers were more than pleased to find in the peddler or storekeeper Jew of Prussia and Bavaria a ready-made scapegoat for their own immensely grown money power.

Pastor Stoecker, with a few well-placed references to the Jewish "moneychangers" of the Gospels and the "thirty pieces of silver" paid to Judas, and the occasional naming of a few known Jewish bankers (e.g., the Rothschilds), knew how to gull a populace apprehensive of the new industrial revolution, to make the average German feel that he needed protection, not from the unnamed new class of money barons and steel magnates, but rather from the "international banker Jew."

Two renowned historians of Stoecker's time, taking a leaf from the pastor's homily, provided detailed dissertations on his simple logic: "The Jew be burned." They were Heinrich von Treitschke and Theodor Mommsen.

In the footsteps of the professors followed thousands of eager students, who made a veritable science out of anti-Semitism. When Adolf Hitler came to power in 1933, the university libraries of Germany could boast of over two thousand volumes on the exciting subject of "Jew Hatred: Why and How." Even foreign countries were affected by this sinful pseudo-historicism, pseudo-economics and pseudo-literature.

While the anti-Semitic passion originated in the Church,

as time went on, propagandists, teachers, artists, and writers, who had not been in a church since baptism joined in lambasting the Jewish character. Many had left their churches long ago, rejecting both the ritual and teaching, but one thing ecclesiastic remained with them: anti-Semitism. They could no longer say the Paternoster, but the hundred anti-Jewish sentences from the New Testament stuck in their minds like sharp nails. Of the dogma of their church they retained little, if anything, except a feeling: The Jew is evil, bloodthirsty, God-killing, money-changing, deceitful (Judas).

Little did they know or care, including the ever-lying clerics, that this brew of hate they were stirring would poison the hearts of their people and one day lead them to massacre a million little children and five million hapless adults of the faith that was holy to Jesus, His mother and father.

In America the billionaire Henry Ford complained that the Jews were money-minded. In England the Cliveden set, which lived in the company of call girls, horse races and night clubs, criticized the Jews for being parasites. In France General Pétain, who betrayed the arms and very soul of his fatherland, attacked the Jews for being internationalists. In Russia Stalin, who drank blood brotherhood with Ribbentrop and Hitler, killed the Jews by the thousands for planning to sell out Communism. In Italy Mussolini, whose titled bankers controlled 90 percent of industry and land holdings, raged against the Jews monopolizing industry. And in Austria Cardinal Innitzer stated with the whole weight of his office as a prince of the Church that the Jews were not to be regarded as citizens of the state.

It seems that every anti-Semite attacks the Jews for his own worldly failings.

STRASBOURG

On St. Valentine's Day (1349) all the Jews in this town were burned alive on their cemetery grounds. The charge, propagated by the clergy, was poisoning Christian wells.

STREET CLEANING

and stable cleaning by Jews on certain days of the month, made compulsory by the ecclesiastical government in Mazara and other cities of Sicily, was discontinued on May 22, 1327, with the abolition of ecclesiastic rule on the island.

Again, the Nazi Germans took an old page from Catholic practice in compelling Jewish citizens, including war veterans and invalid women, to scrub streets and sidewalks with their bare hands.

STUYVESANT, PETER (1592-1672)

Dutch colonial Governor of New Amsterdam, who tried to deport Jewish refugees from the terrors of the Brazilian Inquisition back whence they came because "They are hateful enemies and blasphemous of the name of Christ." (Letter to the West India Company, September 22, 1654.)

SUAREZ, FRANCISCO (1548-1617)

Foremost Spanish Jesuit theologian, who placed "any familiarity with Jews" under strict prohibition; that it should be forbidden to enter a Jewish home; that no Jewish physician might be consulted; that Christians might not bathe with Jews; and that Christian women might not nurse Jewish infants. He also advocated that the Jews should be prohibited from erecting synagogues; that at Passover time they should not be permitted to leave their homes; that the books of the Talmud should be banned.

Suárez was greatly encouraged by Pope Paul V. His influence among Catholic seminarians of the Old and New Worlds is still immense.

SUNDAY SCHOOL

is the fountainhead of the flow of anti-Semitic sentiment. From a current children's text widely used by a major Christian denomination:

"Do not use the expression: "Wicked soldiers with ill-treating Jesus.' Children might identify soldier with wicked. The teacher should not talk of 'wicked soldiers' but 'wicked Jews.'" (*Christian Beliefs and Anti-Semitism*, Glock and Stark.)

From the Sunday school test of the Lutheran Church, Missouri Synod, U.S.A., 1955:

"Give proof that the curse which the Jews called upon their nation still rests on them *and their children* to this very day."

These are just two examples of numerous statements of similar and worse character.

T

TALMUD

The banning of Talmudic literature in the Justinian Christian Code (sixth century) served as a precedent for later accusations by anti-Semites against the "malicious" canon of the Jew.

TECUARA

Anti-Semitic youth group in present-day Argentina, "operating" with strong support of local Catholic clergy.

TISO, MSGR. JOZEF (1887-1947)

Catholic priest, leader of the Slovak Nationalist movement. After Munich, Msgr. Tiso became Premier of autonomous Slovakia. A year later, when the Nazis occupied the truncated shell of the Czechoslovak state, he became President of the "independent" Slovak Republic—"independent" by the grace of Hitler. In emulation of his master, the Monsignor promptly inaugurated a vehement anti-Semitic program in his puppet domain.

TISZA ESZLAR

In this Hungarian town in 1882 a Catholic priest instigated a trial of Jews for ritual blood drinking. This time the prosecution failed; Christianity could no longer employ torture.

TOLEDO

The third council convened in this Spanish city in 589 prohibited Jews from owning Christian slaves, marrying Christian women, or holding any public office. Gregory (saint), the reigning pope, congratulated the assembly on its holy stand against "Jewish perfidy." (Nuremberg Law in its first form.)

TOLLS

See *Judenzoll*.

TOMBSTONES

Jewish cemeteries in Germany, Austria and Poland were ripped off the consecrated grounds and used for military construction as well as for paving streets by the Nazi authorities.

As with many other outrages, the National Socialists

170

had a precedent in the action of Pope Urban VIII (1623-1644) who forbade the Jews to place tombstones on the graves of their beloved. The Pope also ordered all Jewish gravestones ripped out and used in the erection of a city wall.

TORDESILLAS, JUAN DE

This Bishop of Segovia in Spain in 1410 had scores of Jews arrested and executed for breaking consecrated wafers. His vindictiveness knew no bounds. The beautiful synagogue was finally "transformed" into the church of Corpus Christi.

Christians have a talent for creating houses of worship by putting the flock with the Star of David underground and sprinkling holy water on the altar. The latest such transformation occurred in 1966 in Coesfeld, Germany. The synagogue, which escaped Nazi arson during the *Kristallnacht,* has become "Christuskirche" as of this writing.

TORQUEMADA, TOMAS

Dominican confessor of Queen Isabella, who was appointed Inquisitor General of Spain in 1483. Pope Sixtus IV granted permission for secular trials with two Dominicans in charge. The Spanish Inquisition was perhaps the most cynical plot in the black history of Catholicism, aimed at expropriating the property of well-to-do Jews and converts in Spain, for the benefit of the royal court and the Church. Even dead "suspects" had their bones dug up for "trial" so estates could be confiscated from their heirs.

TORTOSA

Site of the most spectacular dialogue, in 1413, between papal representatives and selected rabbis, where the Church held all the aces, including torture screws, the garrote and the torch, with the Jews facing the alternative of either dying spiritually through conversion by an abominable religious clique or dying physically on the pyre.

TOULOUSE

In this French town during the Middle Ages the Jews received a blow on the face each "Good Friday" for killing Jesus. In some other towns special mallets were distributed by the worshipers as a Holy Week ritual signifying the need for punishing the Jewish God killers.

For centuries the local clergy considered this a good way for their flocks to work off "understandable anger." The practice of Good Friday beatings persisted in smaller communities of Europe until the nineteenth century.

TOUSSENEL, ALPHONSE (1803-1885)

Like Karl Marx and Charles Fourier, a "socialist" anti-Semite, he built his case against the Jews on the little legend in the Gospels which depicts the Jews as moneychangers in the Temple.

The Christian churches had so belabored this point, that while nine out of ten Jews were little more than penniless laborers, artisans or peddlers in East Europe, North Africa and the Middle East, Toussenel, like Karl Marx, steadfastly repeated the Christian theme that the Jews were a grasping international group of Christ killers, bent on world hegemony, and therefore each and every one responsible for the sins of all, in space as well as time.

Toussenel noted that the admitted persecution and execution of Jews and their families was to be accepted with satisfaction as just punishment for their unredeemable guilt and as revenge for their arrogant hate of Christian mankind.

He only voiced what had been the Christian attitude from Chrysostom to Pius XII, from Luther to the German Conference of Protestant Bishops.

TOYNBEE, ARNOLD J.

Contemporary English High Church historian, who finds comfort in declaring Jewish martyrdom to be the "deadly recoil on Jewish heads of the shedding of Jesus' blood." The gassing of a million Jewish children in the twentieth century is a "just historic consequence" of an ancestral "crime" of the first century!

Hitler, like the Emperor Titus, appears as the avenging angel of the Lord.

A similar theme is to be found in *A Classical Dictionary* by John Lemprière, D.D., first published in 1788. Here is what the English Doctor of Divinity has to say about the Roman Emperor's destruction of Jerusalem:

"Some authors have reflected with severity upon the cruelties which Titus exercised against the Jews; but though certainly a disgrace to the benevolent features of his character, we must consider him as an instrument in the hands of Providence, exerted for the punishment of a wicked and infatuated people."

Lemprière's dictionary ran through many editions and was widely used in English schools well into the twentieth century, so it may be that Professor Toynbee came upon his deadly cliché ready-made.

TREITSCHKE, HEINRICH VON

Demagogue of nineteenth century Germany, who directed deep-set religious anti-Semitic tendencies into social and economic channels by clever journalistic appeals. He was a pre-Hitler protagonist of the Big Lie. Whatever problem he discussed, Treitschke ended his essays with: "The Jews are our trouble."

TRENT

A famous ritual murder case took place in this Italian town in 1473. A three-year-old boy, Simon, was found dead in the Adige River during Holy Week. The Franciscan friar Bernardinus (sanctified, of course, by the Vatican), a follower of another saint, Bernardinus of Siena, who had warned that the Jews were planning to destroy Christianity through their physicians, incited the mob to bloody excesses after having *predicted* the murder. The Jews of Trent were tried by the bishop. All were burned.

A few years ago the present Bishop of Trent, after having the case thoroughly studied and examined by a legate, publicly admitted the grievous error of the Church in convicting the Jews of Trent. The two murderous Franciscans are still on the holy roster with the rest of the unholy brothers.

We have had in modern times a recurrence of the physician phobia of Saint Bernardinus. Stalin, a former theology student, accused Jewish doctors of planning to destroy Communism by poisoning its leaders.

The Trent trial gave a great impetus to scores of equally false accusations throughout Europe. See also *Vampires*.

TRZECIAK, STANISLAS

Originally professor at the *Catholic Academy of St. Petersburg* during the Nazi era in Warsaw. A malevolent anti-Semite, he pointed out to the Polish clergy the importance of the Jew-baiting encyclical letter of Pope Benedict XIV, who in the eighteenth century enforced Medieval restrictions on the God killers. Prelate Trzeciak in a pastoral letter exclaimed that to fight the Jews was not only a privilege but the duty of every Catholic. Hitler quoted this letter repeatedly.

U

UKRAINIAN ANTI-SEMITISM

in modern years found its theoretician in the executive member of the Communist Academy of Sciences of Kiev, Profim K. Kichko. In his book, *Judaism Without Embellishment,* published by the Academy of Sciences, Kichko, drawing all his arguments from the vast reservoir of Eastern Orthodoxy, declared the Jews to be morally inferior (they betrayed Christ), politically unreliable (they hate the Christian environment) and aiming for control over their Christian comrades.

Significantly, Kichko illustrated his work with anti-Semitic cartoons taken from Church literature of the Czarist period. Kichko has never been removed from his academic position as directing anthropologist at the Kiev University.

UNITED STATES OF AMERICA

is the only one of the Christian nations that never tolerated the torturing, burning, decapitating or hanging of Jews because of their faith. This is simply because the Christian churches in this country never had a right over the life and limb of any resident. Where the Christian churches have wielded power and authority, the Jew has lived under a never-ending threat of religious aggression.

A great number of American colleges are "church-affiliated," however, and therefore prone to anti-Semitism. They refuse to accept Jewish teachers, while employing Christians of any and all denominations. For instance, Agnes Scott College of Atlanta, Georgia, has never in its 78-year history had a Jewish person on its faculty, a record which this Presbyterian institution blandly acknowledges.

This personnel policy, like that of Nazi Germany, is drawn from the rich source of traditional Christian anti-Semitism. I suppose Christ would be rejected as a faculty member, should he apply to the good Presbyters.

The exclusion which has its origin in doctrinal intolerance has also spread to social institutions. A checkup conducted by the Anti-Defamation League in 1966 brought to light that of 505 American country clubs interrogated, 498 would not accept Jewish members—this, after a year of "ecumenism."

USURY

It has been the calculated practice of anti-Semites to charge the Jews with exactly the deed or misdeed they were themselves perpetrating.

Hitler, who sought and almost gained world conquest, charged the Jews with a conspiracy for world control; Henry Ford, who amassed the largest fortune one man has ever possessed, charged the Jews with being money-mad; Queen Isabella of Spain and her consort, who clutched all Spain and more lands than they could manage to their insatiable bosoms, accused the Jews of greed; and Stalin, who spread his spider fingers over the whole globe, denounced the Jewish people for "internationalism."

Who charged the Jews with usury? Let's look at the record.

First, the Catholic Church.

By adopting the legal code of the Hebrews prohibiting any charge for the use of money, Pope Leo I in 443 made the Torah part of the Catholic canon. The ancient Hebrews —shepherds, peasants and fishermen—considered any loan an act of charity, and you don't charge for charity.

The Catholic authorities dominant in all countries prior to the American and French revolutions, tried vainly to apply this Hebrew rule of neighborly generosity to a growing commercial economy, and failed.

In their dilemma the secular rulers of Europe hit upon an obvious way around the prohibition of "interest": "Let the Jews act as the interest brokers; they are not bound by the Catholic canon, neither are they bound by the Hebrew canon in dealing with Christians."

So the Jews became the funnel through which the small but important trade and financial operations were carried on through the Middle Ages. The word "usury" was only used when the Christian creditor, invariably a noble or court personage, was in financial distress and wanted an out. Then king, queen, and feudal lord deserted their "court

176

Jew" and sacrificed him to the mob, with the clergy sounding the necessary anti-Semitic "slogans." It was easy at such times to raise the cry of "Defamer of the host! Vampire, feeding on Christian children's blood! Poisoners of wells! Bringer of the plague! Friend of the Mongols and Saracens! Spitter on the crucifix!"—once the monks and priests began their baying, the pack broke loose.

"Usurer!" was only a minor charge in the hunting call. The word "usurer" meant little to the common man. Up to the era of the French Revolution, the average European was a serf. He had nothing but his hands and, as a pair of hands, was fed enough to keep body and soul together and raise more hands. That ugly expression is still a leftover in our language: a farm hand, a mill hand. Nobody would lend anything to a farmer or artisan or laborer or miner or soldier or clerk. They had nothing, and were nothing until the French Revolution but a chattel of the lord.

However, the lords could profit from trade and manufacturing, and for these operations they needed literate people, people who could write and count; they themselves could not. And they needed men who would do their bidding as tax planners and tax collectors in trade and industry.

They needed more Jews. And they recruited more of them—until the next disaster. Of course, they charged interest for the use of money. The interest was large as the risk was large. In a way, the so-called "usurers" were actually "insurers" of the merchandise, ships and caravans. Since at least one out of every five ships or caravans would fail to return, because of piracy, brigandage, untamed waves or winds, the rates of the lenders were "usurious" by our standards.

Whatever they were, it was the lord's money and the lord's rate. The Jew was only his counselor, his financial adviser, his tax collector, his court Jew.

It is significant that in all the thousandfold expulsions and killings of Jews in the thousand years of the Middle

Ages it was the clergy that inspired the violence and vindictiveness, hardly ever the secular authorities.

And after the expulsion, whatever Jews were found wandering over the dirt roads of Christian Europe were desperately called back by the lords and mayors; they could not manage without the knowledge and planning of the Jews.

The Jew of the Middle Ages was always like a gypsy, close to his wagon. He never knew when some fanatical monk would raise the old cry: "Burn the Christ killers!"

If one town expelled the Jews, they thanked the Lord for the blessing of their life. They pushed on in the darkness of the night, in the ruts of the little-used roads, using their skills whenever and wherever a town or village permitted.

The guilds would not admit them. The Church prohibited all personal contact. Yet the Jews were the artisans of the Middle Ages.

The Jews made horseshoes, nails and plows for the peasants.

The Jews made pots and pans for the women. They made cloaks and doublets for the men. They brewed beer and distilled brandy.

The Jews were dyers and weavers, furriers and stonecutters, engravers and glaziers, shoemakers and saddlers.

They were illuminators of books, armorers and calligraphers.

The Jews lived in small towns where they could serve the people and be out of the eye of the Church hierarchy. And still they could not escape the wrath of the blackclothed ministers of Christ.

The Jew and his pack became proverbial, the wandering Jew a legend. But not a legend of the glory of God, a legend of the vindictiveness in man.

V

The Jews as vampires, ritually ingesting the blood of Christian children, is a lurid image strenuously publicized in the past as well as in the present by the Catholic Church. Vampire accusations against the Jews were first made at the behest of the early Church Fathers in the fourth century, a take-off from a Roman accusation against the early Christians, based on their claim that the Sacrament of the Holy Eucharist involved the real blood of Christ. The charge was repeated for the next fifteen hundred years, leading to ritual-murder trials, torture confessions and the burning of Jews.

Numerous pogroms took place in nineteenth century Russia because the Orthodox clergy accused Jews of blood drinking. Large-scale trials were instigated by the Church in Saratov (1857) and Kutais (1878). The last (Beiliss) trial took place in 1911 at Kiev.

As late as 1881 the official Jesuit journal, *La Civiltà Cattolica*, published a series of articles impugning Jews as vampires: "Such atrocious Hebrew deeds must be founded on some fact, because they excited so much anger of the people."

In an issue of 1892 (No. 8434), joining *Civiltà Cattolica* and other leading Catholic periodicals, the official Vatican newspaper, *Osservatore Romano,* editorialized on the "irrefutable evidence of ritual murder perpetrated by Jews in obedience to the Talmud."

This insinuation was echoed ten years later by a literary organ of the high Anglican Church. In 1911, at the beginning of the Czarist judicial frame-up of the Jew Mendel Beiliss, when the voices of the whole liberal and non-Christian civilized world were raised in protest, the *Oxford and Cambridge Review* called for a ritual trial! The editors were not certain, so they stated, that Jews did not kidnap Christian children and drink their blood at Passover services.

Thus the Church kept the legend of the blood-drinking Jew alive—and ready for the venomous pens of Nazi propagandists, such as Julius Streicher. In his hate-sheet, *Der Stürmer*, Streicher published serial excerpts from Church-inspired ritual murder trials, including the infamous one held at the Italian city of Trent in 1475. Following is one of Streicher's historical gems:

"Also the numerous confessions made by the Jews show that the execution of ritual murders is a law of the Talmud Jew. The former chief rabbi (and later monk) Teofiti declares that the ritual murders take place especially on the Jewish Purim (in memory of the Persian murders) and Passover (in memory of the murder of Christ). The rules are as follows: The blood of the victims is to be tapped by force. On Passover it is to be used in wine and matzos. Thus a small part of the blood is to be poured into the dough of matzos and into the wine. The mixing is done by the head of the Jewish family.

"The procedure is as follows: The family head empties a few drops of the fresh and powdered blood into a glass, wets the fingers of the left hand with it, and sprays (blesses) with it everything on the table. The head of the family then says, 'Thus we ask God to send the ten plagues to all enemies of the Jewish faith.' Then they eat, and at the end the head of the family exclaims, 'May all Gentiles perish, as the child whose blood is contained in the bread and wine.'

"The fresh (or dried and powdered) blood of the slaughtered is further used by young married Jewish couples, by pregnant Jewesses, for circumcision, and so on. Ritual murder is recognized by all Talmud Jews. The Jew believes he absolves himself thus of his sins."

In the early years of Nazism its propagandists at Jewish Easter times, would publish a "warning to the German and Austrian people" to keep their children indoors because of ritual "requirements" of the Jews. (Similar charges that Jews drank the blood of Christian children were re-

180

peated in *The Fascist,* a British paper published prior to World War II.)

Here lies the secret of anti-Semitic brutality, perpetrated directly or indirectly by most of the German Nazis: to the Christian German and Austrian, the Jew was a sinister, vicious killer.

Punishing those "killers," the Christian German considered not a sin but rather his duty. German troops, who might hesitate to brutalize a French or Danish child, would, with the equanimity of their Christian consciences drive a million Jewish children to a ghastly death in the execution chamber.

*

To the astonishment of all, especially the Church, Archbishop Alessandro Gottardi of Trent in Italy acknowledged in October, 1965 the innocence of the Jews in the death of "Little Saint Simon of Trent." In 1475 twelve Jews had been executed for the crime after indescribable tortures to make them all confess.

The research to clear the unfortunate Jewish victims was conducted by the Reverend P. Eckert and appeared in the *Trentine Studies of Historical Science.* Upon publication of this extensive study, the Congregation of Rites forbade the veneration of relics or saying of Masses in Simon's name.

Father Eckert's conclusion after years of examination of the "evidence" in the archives of Trent, Rome and Vienna is that the trial of Trent had ended in judicial murder.

In spite of repeated requests by Jewish and liberal spokesmen, Pope Paul VI refused to open the hundreds of similar assassinations of Jews as vampires to the critical eyes of objective researchers. Thus the monstrous accusations against the Hebrew people will remain enshrined in the history books, chapels, monuments, and hagiography of the Church. The vampire Jew lives on in Catholic Europe to haunt the dreams of Christian children and childish women and men.

VATICAN APPOINTEES

Cardinals, Bishops and sundry Prelates within the Nazi domain were far from neutral or silent onlookers of the "Brown Scene."

Already the Concordat of Collaboration of July 20, 1933, entered into by Dr. Pacelli of the Vatican and the Hitler Government (article 30) ordered that on all Sundays and Holidays in all Churches of the Reich the religious services be concluded with a prayer for the "National Socialist Realm." Cardinal Faulhaber of Munich delivered a sermon in 1936 claiming the Pope to be the best, perhaps the only friend of the new "German Reich."

On June 23, 1950, at the "Catholic Day" at Bonn Cardinal Frings, of Cologne, as first German Prelate, demanded the rearmament of Hitler Germany. As late as 1967 Frings was involved in anti-Semitic utterances.

In June 1933 Germany's Catholic bishops published a communal pastoral letter which emphasized: "We German Bishops do not wish to underestimate or even hinder the 'National Resurgence' of the New Reich." Thus, individually and by hand, underwrote all German Cardinals, Archbishops and Bishops in 1933, the year of Hitler's ascension.

On August 1933 Archbishop Gröber, who later joined the Nationalist Socialist Party as a regular member, ordained: "I see no obstacle in placing the Nazi Flag and the Hooked Cross into the sanctuary of every Catholic Church."

On July 10th of the same year Bishop Vogt of Aachen promised by telegram to cooperate with the New Order.

Bishop Berning of Osnabrück declared all German Prelates would support Hitler's State with "warm love and all their power." Bishop Bornewasser of Trier exclaimed: "With head high and strong step will we enter the New Order and serve it with all our strength and soul."

Bishop Burger asserted: "The aims of the Hitler Reich are since long ago the aims of the Catholic Church (sic!)."

Prelate Steinmann of Berlin deliriously yelled: "Our

chancellor was called by God Himself." Cardinal Faulhaber implored the American Cardinals Hayes of New York and Mundelein of Chicago (1934) to stop the libelling of Hitler in the American press. Faulhaber wrote at the same time to the new chancellor: "Your handclasp with the Vatican implies the greatest moral deed of history, a majestic achievement and innumerable blessings."

In June 1936 Bishop Berning inspected the Concentration Camps of Emsland. The good Bishop praised the diligence of Himmler (sic!) and said: "All those who doubt the future of the New Germany should be brought here."

In 1937 Archbishop Gröber published a "Handbook of Religious Problems of the Day," in which widely quoted Catholic theologians emphasize "Hitler's Reich as a State of Law and Order and as a Defense of European Culture."

On March 12, 1938, the Catholic hierarchy of Austria, under the leadership of Cardinal Innitzer, welcomed Hitler's invading troops with ringing of all church bells and placing of Hooked Cross Nazi Flags at the church altars and gates.

Archbishop Weitz of Salzburg published on March 28, 1938, a "Solemn Declaration" that the thousand year long yearning of the Austrian Church had been fulfilled with the advent of Hitler in Austria.

In the same year the Bishops Conference in Fulda sent Hitler a congratulatory telegram on the capitulation of the Czech government at the same time ordering all Church bells to ring the next Sunday.

In every Catholic Diocese Hitler's 50th birthday was celebrated with the Praying of the "Pater Noster," bell ringing and raising of Nazi Flags before the Altar.

Archbishop Jäger of Paderborn called the war against the allies a struggle in defense of Christianity; Bishop Rackl of Eichstätt referred to Hitler's attacks as a holy crusade and Bishop Galen expressed again and again hope for a German victory.

In the war against the allies the Austrian archbishop Ferdinand von Seckau spoke (1944) of Hitler's "heroic deeds," and Archbishop Kolb of Bamberg cried: Behind our army of soldiers stands an army of devotionally praying Germans. (January 31, 1944.) Further Kolb: *"Christ expects that obedient as He was we too willingly take upon us the Cross."*

So wrote a Catholic Bishop in 1944 of the Beast of Berlin, killer of a million Jewish children.

VATICAN LINE

This was the name given a group of Catholic clerics in Rome, led by Bishop Alois Hudal, who in the early years after Hitler's war helped Nazi elite members, among them Eichmann, to escape to Argentina. The Vatican Line ceased functioning in 1949.

Bishop Alois Hudal, Rector of the German Church in Rome during the Hitler era, called the Nuremberg Laws "unavoidable countermeasures" against "alien" elements.

VENGEANCE

"This is a time for vengeance on the Jewish serfs and vagabonds for what they did to our Lord Jesus. Let us stamp out their houses and their brood and burn their synagogues and talmuds."—Martin Luther

"Let us take vengeance on the Jewish beasts for what they did to German folkdom and pitilessly wipe out the foul brood."—General von Reichenau, 1941

VENICE

On December 3, 1943, the Cardinal Patriarch of Venice lodged a complaint with the German Consul General that the Italian authorities had failed to arrest all Jews in their drive to segregate non-Aryans. The cordial wish and desire of the Patriarch was to have all Jews behind ghetto bars to assure their extermination once and for all.

VESPASIAN

The Roman Caesar threw legion after legion into the war against the Jews. He pleaded with them, as did his son Titus, for a token surrender, guaranteeing their freedom except for the minimum of Roman sovereignty and Caesar's bust in the vestry.

The Jews had accepted the rule of their land by foreign despots backed by overwhelming power, but never desecration of their Temple. They would rather see it go up in flames, and they did.

And these were the same Jews who are supposed to have traded cows and sheep in their house of worship! So says the Gospel spread by Roman Bishops to discredit the Jews, who would rather give up their souls than their faith.

The Catholics thus marked the Jews as godless moneychangers. But the only change made by the Jews of Jerusalem was into armor. And so died a half-million men that their God might live.

VICHY FRANCE

The *Semaine Religieuse* of the d'Evreux diocese, at the request of regional propaganda staff officials, agreed to publish a communique justifying the Vichy measures taken against the Jews, using a similar edict of Pope Paul IV as their justification.

VIENNA

On March 12, 1421, Duke Albrecht V of Austria had 210 Jews, men, women and children, burned alive for refusal to accept conversion to Christianity. For decades thereafter, the Jews called Austria "Bloodland." Little did they know that five hundred years later the Austrians would kill and burn a thousand times this many Jews, with Cardinal Innitzer blessing the dominant hooked cross.

In 1610 the medical faculty at the Catholic University

185

of Vienna announced that every Jewish physician was bound by his faith to kill every tenth Christian patient.

Bishop Kollonitsch of Vienna "inspired" the destruction of the great synagogue in his city. After the expulsion of all the Viennese Jews by Leopold I on July 25, 1670, St. Margaret's Church was erected on the ruins of the Hebrew temple, following the thousand-year-old precedent established by the clergy.

As late as 1760 Empress Maria Theresa of Austria ordered that all Jews wear a yellow badge on their left arm. Hitler's Gauleiter repeated this Catholic order almost two hundred years later.

W

WANDERING JEW

Legendary figure who taunted Christ on the way to Golgotha. As punishment, he was condemned to live without rest or end. He was reported alive in 1227 by no less an authority than an Armenian archbishop. This confirmation was widely hailed by the learned Catholic clergy of the time.

WELL POISONING

by Jews was an accusation given wide credence by Church authorities, especially in the fourteenth century. In 1348 the Jews of Provence were burned as well poisoners. In Germany they were even accused of poisoning the Christian air! The spread of leprosy was attributed to them, and suspects were tortured to provide "verification." In 1679 Abraham a Santa Clara accused the Jews of Venice of having "caused" the pestilence.

WET-NURSING

In 1205 Pope Innocent III, in a letter to the Bishop of Paris, accused the Jews of pouring the milk of Christian women nursing their children into latrines during Easter-time. Christian women should therefore not enter the service of these hateful disbelievers.

A law prohibiting Christian women from serving as nurses in Jewish homes was promulgated in 1581 by Pope Gregory XIII in his bull *Antiqua Judaeorum*.

WHOSE HOLY CITY?

May, 1967, witnessed one of the most dramatic exhibitions of the persistent Christian gospel prejudice against the children of Israel. When fourteen Arab nations, with a population of over a hundred million bristling under Egyptian incitement, surrounded the little Jewish state with thousands of tanks, planes, cannons and missiles, they threatened the Jewish people in the Middle East not just with war, but with extermination.

"We shall liquidate the Jews," came the voice of Radio Amman; "After this war, there will be no Jewish survivors in Israel," echoed the commander of the Arab "Liberation Front," Achmed Shukairy; "We are prepared to annihilate Israel," exclaimed Jordan's King Hussein; "We shall destroy Israel," responded Nasser.

Yet, with all these public proclamations of impending genocide, in the United States of America not a single Christian clergyman, minister or priest, bishop or cardinal, raised his hand or voice to stop the expected slaughter of a small and ancient people!

The Christian churches maintained silence, the silence of a cemetery. The silence that prevailed when Hitler brutally proclaimed in print and spoken word: "I shall kill all Jews, men, women and children."

Shukairy, like Hitler, was outspoken and sincere in his hate which was amplified by modern communication media into apocalyptic thunder. The hellish intent of both was loud and clear, yet no Christian churchman heard their threat.

Yet, when tiny Israel gathered its forces and swiftly as the Dark Angel smote the war chariots of the Egyptians with man and horse and wagon, *then,* and only then, did our Christian ministers of the Lord regain their hearing and sight—and voice! All over America they trumpeted: The Jews must leave all the occupied lands and especially, very especially so, the Old City of Jerusalem.

It was all right for the Moslem King of Jordan to have been master of the Holy City for twenty years, but no Jew should rule the city of Jerusalem!

These clergymen know that the democratic citizens of Israel will certainly govern the old city with keener judgment than any Arab sheikh, but it seems no Christian clergyman can stand by silently while the anti-Semitic pronouncements of the New Testament, of the eternal banishment of the Jews from the Holy Land, are brought to nought; none can bear to see the city of Jerusalem, where "no stone be left upon the other," reborn and glorified, as never before, by Jewish hands.

To the custodians of the biased books of the New Testament, the land and faith of the Jew is accursed, and must remain thus in eternity as "just" punishment for *the* Jews' guilt of Jesus' crucifixion.

The New Testament demands the Jew to be a pariah forever, and the coming glory of an all-Jewish Jerusalem is a curse and blasphemy to the upholders of this Testament.

Could it be that the hate of the Jew is the core of the New Testament, deeper than the tepid "love of mankind" professed so often, but so selectively?

"The Jew may not rule the Holy City." This fiat, sent out by the Vatican when Israeli soldiers were still at the gate of the old city, was echoed by the Protestant World Council of Churches and the sundry Orthodox Patriarchs and Coptic dignitaries.

One truth they all tremble to face: If Israel holds the Holy City, then the great message of the gospel, the "guilt" of the Jew and his perennial punishment, is rendered patently false and comes back on the heads of the Church fathers, past and present, who have propagated it for 1800 years.

WORMS

The whole Jewish population of this German town was killed by the first Crusader bands, incited by such preachers as Peter the Hermit, a saintly figure in all Catholic history books.

Y

YELLOW BADGE

See *Gelbe Fleck*.

Z

ZENO, SAINT

Bishop of the fourth century, who bewailed the circumstance that when inspired monks invaded Jewish homes and killed the resisting inhabitants, they burned only the corpses. He meant that the Jews still living also should have been given to the flames for the greater glory of Jesus.

Selected Bibliography of Readily Available Documentation

Adler, H. G., *Die Juden in Deutschland: Von der Aufklärung bis zum Nationalsozialismus*

Andics, Hellmut, *Der Ewige Jude: Ursachen und Geschichte des Antisemitismus*

Baum, Gregory, *Is the New Testament Anti-Semitic?*

Berdyaev, Nicolas, *Christianity and Anti-Semitism*

Bernstein, Peretz F., *Jew-Hate As a Sociological Problem*

Blumenkranz, Bernhard, *Le Juif Médiéval au Miroir de l'art Chrétien*

Buchheim, Hans, *Das Dritte Reich*

Celnik, Max and Isaac, *A Bibliography on Judaism and Jewish-Christian Relations*

Cohn, Norman, *Warrant for Genocide*

Corsten, W., *Kölner Aktenstücke zur Lage der katholischen Kirche in Deutschland* 1933-1945

Coudenhove-Kalergi, Count Heinrich, *Anti-Semitism Throughout the Ages*

Daane, James, *The Anatomy of Anti-Semitism and Other Essays on Religion and Race*

De Haas, Jacob, *The Encyclopedia of Jewish Knowledge*

Deschner, Karlheinz, *Das Jahrhundert der Barbarei*

————, *Mitt Gott und den Faschisten*

Duquesne, Jacques, *Les Catholiques français sous l'occupation*

Eckert, Willehad Paul, *Judenhass—Schuld der Christen?*

Esh, Benzion Dinur Shaul, *Yad Washem Studies on the European Jewish Catastrophe and Resistance*

Falconi, Carlo, *Das Schweigen des Papistes*

Flannery, Edward H., *The Anguish of the Jews*

Friedländer, Saul, *Auftakt zum Untergang*

———, *Pius XII and the Third Reich*
Glock, Charles Y., and Stark, Rodney, *Christian Beliefs and Anti-Semitism*
Hargrove, Katharine T., *The Star and the Cross*
Hay, Malcolm, *Europe and the Jews: The Pressure of Christendom on the People of Israel for 1900 Years*
Heer, Friedrich, *Gottes erste Liebe*
Hegner, H. S., *Die Reichskanzlei 1933-1945*
Hilberg, Raul, *The Destruction of the European Jews*
Huss, Hermann, and Schröder, Andreas, eds., *Antisemitismus zur Pathologie der bürgerlichen Gesellschaft*
Hyamson, Albert M., and Silbermann, A. M., eds., *Vallentine's Jewish Encyclopaedia*
Isaac, Jules, *The Teaching of Contempt: Christian Roots of Anti-Semitism*
Katz, Robert, *Death in Rome*
Knight, George A. F., *Jews and Christians: Preparation for Dialogue*
Kuhner, Hans, *Encyclopedia of the Papacy*
Lebreton, Jules, and Zeiller, Jacques, *The History of the Primitive Church*
Lewy, Guenter, *Die katholische Kirche und das Dritte Reich*
Livingston, Sigmund, *Must Men Hate?*
Marcus, Jacob R., *The Jew in the Medieval World*
Marx, Karl, *A World Without Jews*
Mosse, Werner E., *Entscheidungsjahr 1932*
Müller, Hans, *Katholische Kirche und Nationalsozialismus*
Munck, J., *Christus und Israel*
Noller, Sonja, and von Kotze, Hildegard, *Faksimile— Querschnitt durch den Völkischen Beobachter*
Olson, Bernhard E., *Faith and Prejudice*
Parkes, James, *The Foundations of Judaism and Christianity*
Plaidy, Jean, *The Spanish Inquisition*
Poliakov, Léon, *The History of Anti-Semitism*
Poliakov, Léon and Wulf, Josef, *Das Dritte Reich und die Juden*
Raisin, Jacob S., *Gentile Reactions to Jewish Ideals*

191

Reck-Malleczewen, Friedrich Percyval, *Tagebuch eines Verzweifelten*

Roth, Cecil, *History of the Marranos*

Runes, Dagobert, D., *The Jew and the Cross*

Rynne, Xavier, *The Fourth Session: The Debates and Decrees of Vatican Council II, September 14 to December 8, 1965*

Sachar, Abram Leon, *A History of the Jews*

Samuel, Maurice, *Blood Accusation: The Strange History of the Beiliss Case*

Shirer, William L., *The Rise and Fall of the Third Reich: A History of Nazi Germany*

Silberner, Edmund, *Sozialisten zur Judenfrage: Ein Beitrag zur Geschichte des Sozialismus vom Anfang des 19 Jahrhunderts bis 1914*

Singer, Isidore, ed., *The Jewish Encyclopedia*

Synan, Edward A., *The Popes and the Jews in the Middle Ages*

Tetens, T. H., *The New Germany and the Old Nazis*